**olive**
magazine

# 101 SEASONAL TREATS

3 5 7 9 10 8 6 4 2

Published in 2007 by BBC Books, an imprint of Ebury Publishing

Ebury Publishing is a division of the Random House Group

First published 2007
Copyright © 2007
All photographs © *olive* magazine 2007

Lulu Grimes has asserted her right to be identified as the author of this
work in accordance with the Copyright, Designs and Patents Act 1988

The Random House Group Limited Reg. No. 954009

Addresses for companies within the Random House Group can be found at
www.randomhouse.co.uk

A CIP catalogue record for this book is available from the British Library

The Random House Group Limited makes every effort to ensure that the
papers used in our books are made from trees that have been legally
sourced from well-managed and credibly certified forests. Our paper
procurement policy can be found at www.randomhouse.co.uk

Commissioning Editor: Vivien Bowler    Project Editor: Laura Nickoll
Designer: Kathryn Gammon    Production Controller: Peter Hunt

Printed and bound in Italy by LEGO SpA
Colour origination by Dot Gradations Ltd, UK

ISBN-13: 978 0 563 49396 9

# 101 SEASONAL TREATS

feel-good food for all year round

Editor
**Lulu Grimes**

BOOKS

# Contents

# Introduction

At *olive* we enjoy using seasonal ingredients because they give the food year a distinct rhythm and make the most of food when it is at its very best. As more and more seasonal ingredients are available from shops and markets and via the delivery of fruit and veg boxes, eating seasonally also provides the chance to try out new recipes, using produce that you may not have been able to buy before to cook for yourself.

Seasonality provides the opportunity not only to eat what seems right at any particular time of year – strawberries really do taste better in summer and roasted root vegetables are far more appealing in winter – but also to take advantage of seasonal 'gluts'. Berries, asparagus and wild mushrooms suddenly become affordable to eat in quantity, and every day if that is what you feel like. For this collection the *olive* food team have picked out 101 easy, achievable recipes, such as *Chicken with saffron and chilli*, pictured opposite (see page 84 for the recipe), to enjoy across the whole year, season by season.

As always, all the recipes have been thoroughly tested in the *olive* kitchen to make sure that they taste fabulous and work for you first time.

Lulu Grimes
*olive* magazine

# Notes and Conversions

## NOTES ON THE RECIPES

• Where possible, we use humanely reared meats, free-range chickens and eggs, and unrefined sugar.

• Eggs are large unless stated otherwise. Pregnant women, elderly people, babies and toddlers, and anyone who is unwell should avoid eating raw and partially cooked eggs.

## APPROXIMATE WEIGHT CONVERSIONS

• All the recipes in this book are listed with metric measurements.

• Cup measurements, which are used by cooks in Australia and America, have not been listed here as they vary from ingredient to ingredient. Please use kitchen scales to measure dry/solid ingredients.

## OVEN TEMPERATURES

| gas | °C | fan °C | °F | description |
| --- | --- | --- | --- | --- |
| ¼ | 110 | 90 | 225 | Very cool |
| ½ | 120 | 100 | 250 | Very cool |
| 1 | 140 | 120 | 275 | Cool or slow |
| 2 | 150 | 130 | 300 | Cool or slow |
| 3 | 160 | 140 | 325 | Warm |
| 4 | 180 | 160 | 350 | Moderate |
| 5 | 190 | 170 | 375 | Moderately hot |
| 6 | 200 | 180 | 400 | Fairly hot |
| 7 | 220 | 200 | 425 | Hot |
| 8 | 230 | 210 | 450 | Very hot |
| 9 | 240 | 220 | 475 | Very hot |

## SPOON MEASURES

• Spoon measurements are level unless otherwise specified.

• 1 teaspoon (tsp) = 5ml

• 1 tablespoon (tsp) = 15ml

• 1 Australian tablespoon = 20ml (cooks in Australia should measure 3 teaspoons where 1 tablespoon is specified in a recipe)

## APPROXIMATE LIQUID CONVERSIONS

| metric | imperial | US |
| --- | --- | --- |
| 60ml | 2fl oz | ¼ cup |
| 125ml | 4fl oz | ½ cup |
| 175ml | 6fl oz | ¾ cup |
| 225ml | 8fl oz | 1 cup |
| 300ml | 10fl oz/½ pint | 1¼ cups |
| 450ml | 16fl oz | 2 cups/1 pint |
| 600ml | 20fl oz/1 pint | 2½ cups |
| 1 litre | 35fl oz/1¾ pints | 1 quart |

Please note that an Australian cup is 250ml, ¾ cup is 190ml, ½ cup is 125ml, ¼ cup is 60ml.

# Sweet potato and carrot soup with chilli oil

50 minutes

**olive oil**

**onion** 1 large, chopped

**sweet potatoes** 750g, peeled and evenly chunked

**carrots** 250g, peeled and evenly chunked

**vegetable or chicken stock** powder or cubes, made up to 1.5 litres

**chilli oil** to serve

■ Heat 4 tbsp olive oil in a large saucepan and gently fry the onion over a medium heat until softened but not browned. Add the sweet potato and carrots and cook, covered, for 10 minutes or so, until the vegetables are glistening and starting to soften.

■ Pour in the stock, bring to the boil and then simmer, covered, for 30 minutes until the vegetables are tender. Pour into a blender (if you use a processor you won't get as velvety a texture) and whiz until smooth – do this in batches if you need to. Return to the pan and gently reheat, seasoning to taste with salt, freshly ground black pepper and a touch of chilli oil. **Serves 4–6**

Sweet potatoes add a depth of flavour to carrots that have been stored over the winter.

# Mussels with coriander cream

30 minutes

---

**mussels** 2kg, cleaned with any beards
    removed
**butter**
**onion** 1, finely chopped
**garlic** 4 cloves, finely chopped
**white wine**
**single cream** 142ml carton
**coriander** a large handful of leaves,
    roughly chopped

■ Throw away any broken mussels or open ones that don't close after a tap on the sink. Melt a large knob of butter in a large saucepan and cook the onion and garlic for a minute or 2 until transparent and soft.

■ Turn up the heat, tip in the mussels with a good slosh of wine then cover and cook for 3 minutes or until all the shells have opened – throw away any that don't. Pour in the cream and stir well, throw in the coriander, season and serve in large bowls. **Serves 6**

You'll need to use a large pan to give all the mussels enough space to open.

# Grilled goat's cheese with red potatoes

**35 minutes**

---

**red-skinned potatoes** 500g, small ones
**olive oil**
**firm goat's cheese** 200g
**pesto** 4 tbsp

You'll need a goat's cheese that is firm to the touch; anything too soft will melt too quickly.

■ Steam or simmer the potatoes for 15–20 minutes until tender. When cool enough to handle, cut into slices. Heat the grill. On a lightly oiled baking sheet, overlap the potato slices to make 4 circles, finishing with a slice on top of each. Drizzle with a little oil and grill for 4–5 minutes. Slice the goat's cheese into 4 rounds and put a slice on each potato circle. Brown under the grill for 4–5 minutes.

■ Thin the pesto with a little oil if necessary; it needs to be spoonable. Using a fish slice, carefully transfer each potato circle to a plate and drizzle with pesto. Season with salt flakes and freshly ground black pepper. **Serves 4**

# Home-cured organic salmon with beetroot

30 minutes + 1–3 days in the fridge

**organic salmon fillet** in one piece, skin on, about 500g
**Maldon sea salt** 1 ½ tbsp
**golden granulated sugar** 1 tbsp
**light muscovado sugar** 1 tbsp
**mustard powder** 1 tbsp
**ground mace** a pinch
**cooked beetroot** (without vinegar) 2, thinly sliced
**crème fraîche** 200g carton, mixed with a handful each of chopped mint and dill
**rye bread** to serve

■ Rinse the salmon and pat it dry. Rub the flat of your hand over the surface of the fish and pull out any little bones with a pair of tweezers. Lay a sheet of foil, large enough to wrap to wrap the fish completely, on a tray and put the salmon on it, skin-side down.

■ Combine the salt, sugars and spices and rub over the salmon. Lay the beetroot slices over the fish and wrap the foil tightly around it. Put a board on top and weigh it down with heavy objects such as tin cans. Chill in the fridge for at least 24 hours and up to 3 days. A puddle of deep-purple liquid will form in the tray – tip this out as it collects.

■ When you're ready to serve, remove the foil and scrape off the beetroot and spices mixture. Thinly slice the salmon and serve with rye bread and the herbed crème fraîche. **Serves 4**

The beetroot adds a delicate flavour as well as a pretty pink edging to the salmon slices.

# Soft-boiled egg with purple-sprouting broccoli

30 minutes

purple sprouting broccoli, stems trimmed
and peeled if tough
eggs 4
butter 50g
anchovy fillets 4

■ Steam the broccoli until tender, about 5–8 minutes depending on how thick the stems are. Meanwhile boil the eggs for 4 minutes (longer if you would like them harder).

■ Melt the butter in a small pan and add the anchovy fillets. Cook over a low heat, stirring until they've dissolved into the butter. Season with pepper. Toss the broccoli in the anchovy butter and serve it to dip in the eggs. **Serves 4**

You can also use duck eggs. They are richer and will need 3 minutes cooking.

# Spicy lamb and prunes on pistachio couscous

30 minutes

**ready-to-eat prunes** 100g, roughly chopped

**couscous** 100g

**boiling hot vegetable stock** fresh, cubes or liquid, made up to 150ml

**lamb neck fillet** about 350g, cut into thick slices

**harissa** 1 tbsp

**pistachio nuts** 50g, shelled and roughly chopped

**mint** a handful of leaves, chopped

**lemon wedges** to serve

■ Put the prunes in a mug and just cover with boiling water. In a bowl, pour the hot stock over the couscous, cover and put to one side. Mix the lamb with the harissa.

■ Heat a dry frying pan and cook the pistachios until just starting to brown. Tip them out of the pan and add the lamb. Fry for 2–3 minutes each side, until well browned. Add the prunes and their water and bubble up, stirring and scraping until the lamb is cooked through. Mix the pistachios with the couscous and serve topped with the lamb, prunes and mint, with the lemon wedges to squeeze over. **Serves 2**

Harissa can vary in strength, so don't be tempted to add more unless you know how strong it is.

# Roasted sea bream with lemon and basil

## 45 minutes

**olive oil**

**garlic** 4 cloves, bashed

**lemons** 2, cut into wedges

**fennel** 2 bulbs, cut into wedges

**red chilli** 2 whole, split lengthways from the stalk

**sea bream or sea bass** 2 large or 3 medium, cleaned and scaled

**basil** 1 bunch, roughly chopped

■ Heat the oven to 200°C/fan 180°C/gas 6. Slosh some olive oil into a roasting tin and tip in the garlic, lemon, fennel and chilli. Put the tin in the oven for 20–25 minutes to start everything roasting.

■ Take out the tin and turn the oven down to 180°C/fan 160°C/gas 4. Make several slashes on both sides of the fish. Push the lemon pieces to the edge of the tin and put the fish on top of the vegetables. Drizzle over some more olive oil and season well. Put back in the oven for 15–20 minutes or until the fish is cooked through – it should feel firm and look flaky through its skin. Scatter over the basil. **Serves 6**

Look out for lemons from Sicily as the season starts in spring.

# Mediterranean guinea fowl

55 minutes

olive oil

**pancetta** 4 thick slices

**guinea fowl** 1, cut into 8 pieces

**banana shallots** (the long ones) 2,
    quartered

**garlic** 2 cloves, finely sliced

**roasted red and yellow peppers** from
    a jar, 100g, drained

**black and green olives** 3 tbsp

**young carrots** 8, trimmed

**bay leaves** 2

**white wine** 300ml

■ Heat the oven to 190°C/fan 170°C/gas 5.
Heat 1 tbsp oil in a large, shallow
ovenproof pan. Cook the pancetta on
each side until golden, then remove. Add
the guinea fowl to the pan in batches
and brown all over. Remove and set aside.

■ Add the shallots and fry for 3 minutes;
add the garlic and cook for a further
1 minute. Remove from the heat and
return the pancetta and guinea fowl to
the pan with the peppers, olives, carrots
and bay leaves. Pour over the wine,
season and cook uncovered in the oven
for 40 minutes until cooked through.

**Serves 4**

New season carrots are small enough to
use whole in this recipe.

# Red spring onion and Serrano ham tart

1 hour

olive oil

butter

**red spring onions** 3 bunches, ends
   trimmed

**balsamic vinegar** ½ tbsp

**caster sugar** 1 tsp

**ready-roll puff pastry** 375g packet

**Serrano ham** 8 slices

**egg** 1, beaten with a splash of cold water

■ Heat 1 tbsp olive oil and a large knob
of butter in a large frying pan, add the
spring onions with the vinegar and
sugar, and cook for 1 minute, turning
them once. Set aside.

■ Heat the oven to 180°C/fan 160°C/gas 4
and put a baking sheet in the oven.
Lightly oil another baking sheet and
unroll the puff pastry on to it. Using a
sharp knife, score a line all round the
pastry, 1.5cm in from the edge. Lay the
ham within the line and put the spring
onions on top in 2 rows (you may have to
trim to fit). Season well. Brush the pastry
border with egg, then fold the edges in
to meet the scored line. Brush the new
border with egg. Put the baking sheet on
top of the one already in the oven and
bake for 30 minutes until golden brown.

**Serves 4**

Red spring onions are in season now.
They have an intense ruby hue that
grows brighter with cooking, but if you
can't find any, green ones are also good.

# Springtime shepherd's pie

**50 minutes + 20 minutes in the oven**

**potatoes** 1.5kg
**lamb mince** 500g
**leeks** 2, thinly sliced
**spring onions** 4, sliced
**carrots** 2, diced
**celery** 1 stick, diced
**courgette** 1, diced
**half-fat crème fraîche** 200ml carton
**lemon** 1, zest
**butter** 50g
**milk** 100ml
**parsley** 1 bunch, leaves only, chopped
**chives** 1 bunch, chopped

■ Heat the oven to 190°C/fan 170°C/gas 5. Boil the potatoes until tender (about 15 minutes), then drain thoroughly.

■ Meanwhile, heat a large frying pan and cook the mince, breaking it up with a wooden spoon, until browned – unless the mince is very lean, you shouldn't need to add any oil. Add the leek, spring onion, carrot and celery and cook, stirring, for 3 minutes, until beginning to soften. Stir in the courgette, crème fraîche and the lemon zest. Taste and season.

■ Heat the milk and ¾ of the butter in a pan, add the potatoes and mash until smooth. Stir in the herbs and season with a little salt. Put the lamb mixture into an ovenproof dish and pile the potato on top, spreading it out to cover the meat completely. Dot with the rest of the butter and bake for 20 minutes until golden on top. **Serves 6**

Lightening a winter dish like this with veg works brilliantly; you could also add frozen peas if you like.

# Chicken with spring herbs

**20 minutes + 20 minutes in the oven**

---

**chervil leaves** a handful, finely chopped
**parsley** ½ bunch or pack, finely chopped
**mint** 2 tbsp leaves, chopped
**mascarpone** 250g carton
**chicken breasts** 4, skin-on
**leeks** 6 **or spring onions** 12, sliced
   lengthways
**white wine** 1 glass
**butter** 25g

■ Heat the oven to 180°C/fan 160°C/gas 4. Mix the herbs with the mascarpone and season well. Lift the skin carefully off the chicken breasts and spread a quarter of the mixture on each breast. Put the skin back down and smooth it carefully over the mascarpone.

■ Put the leeks or spring onions in a baking dish, cut-side up, and pour over the white wine. Season. Arrange the chicken on top of the vegetables, skin-side up. Dot the butter over the chicken and leeks and roast for 20 minutes until the chicken is golden and crisp and the leeks tender. **Serves 4**

Roasting chicken breasts on top of vegetables and wine helps keep them succulent by crisping the tops but steaming the underneath.

# Grilled sardines with paprika

10 minutes + 8 minutes under the grill

**sardines** 4 large or 8 small, gutted
**garlic** 2 cloves, crushed
**olive oil**
**smoked paprika** ½ tbsp
**lemon wedges** to serve

■ Heat the grill to its highest setting. Rinse the sardines and pat them dry. Take off the heads if you prefer. Make 3 deep slashes on both sides of each fish with a sharp knife. Mix the garlic with the olive oil and paprika to make a thin paste. Rub the paste into both sides of the sardines, pushing it into the slashes.

■ Put the sardines on a lightly oiled baking sheet. Grill for 3–4 minutes on each side, depending on how big they are. Season with salt flakes and freshly milled black pepper and serve with lemon wedges to squeeze over. **Serves 4**

Sardines are a brilliant fish for everyday eating: cheap, easy to cook and full of flavour.

# Spring greens and blue cheese risotto

## 40 minutes

**spring greens or spinach** 500g, roughly
chopped

**olive oil**

**butter**

**onion** 1, finely chopped

**garlic** 2 cloves, finely chopped

**risotto rice** 400g

**white wine** 150ml

**chicken stock** fresh, cube or powder
made up to 600ml, hot

**flat-leaf parsley** chopped, 4 tbsp

**blue cheese** (such as Dolcelatte) 150g,
crumbled

**pine nuts** 25g, toasted

Spring greens can be tough so strip out
any woody stalks and leathery leaves
before you start.

■ Boil 600ml water with a pinch of salt
and cook the greens for 1 minute. Drain,
reserving the liquid. Heat a large pan and
add the oil and butter. Heat until the
butter is foaming then add the onion
and cook gently for about 5 minutes until
soft. Add the garlic and cook for a further
2 minutes. Stir in the rice and heat
through for a few minutes until the
grains are shiny and coated. Pour in the
wine and cook over a high heat for 1
minute, stirring constantly.

■ Turn down the heat to medium and
stir in the liquid from the spring greens,
a ladleful at a time, allowing it to be
absorbed before adding more. When the
liquid is used up, continue the process
with hot stock. It should take 20 minutes.

■ When the texture is creamy, but each
grain is still firm to the bite, the risotto is
ready. Take off the heat and stir in the
greens, parsley, cheese, pine nuts. Season.
Leave to rest with the lid off for a few
minutes then serve immediately. **Serves 4**

# Purple-sprouting broccoli and sausage tarts

40 minutes

ready-roll puff pastry 375g
purple sprouting broccoli 250g
olive oil
Italian-style pork sausages 400g, skins removed and broken into chunks
fennel seeds 1 tsp (look in the spice section)
dried crushed chillies 1 tsp
Parmesan cheese grated, 4 tbsp
cherry tomatoes 200g, cut in half
mozzarella cheese 2 balls (250g), drained and torn into pieces
basil leaves a small handful, torn

Blanching purple-sprouting broccoli before using helps to keep the bright-green colour.

■ Cut the pastry to make 4 squares. Put on baking parchment and pop in the freezer for 10 minutes. Heat the oven to 200°C/fan 180°C/gas 6 and put in two large baking sheets. Cut the broccoli into pieces and blanch for 2 minutes in salted, boiling water. Rinse in cold water and drain well. Heat a non-stick pan with 1 tbsp olive oil and fry the sausage, fennel seeds and chillies until the sausage is browned all over.

■ Keep each pastry square on the parchment paper and arrange the broccoli over the pastry leaving a 2cm border. Divide the sausage, Parmesan and tomato among the tarts. Remove the baking sheets from the oven and slide the tarts off the paper on to the hot trays. Bake for 20–25 minutes until the pastry is puffed and golden. In the last couple of minutes of cooking, top each tart with mozzarella and let it melt. Remove from the oven and scatter over the basil. Serve warm. **Serves 4**

# Slow-roasted Tuscan pork with roast garlic mash

15 minutes + 5 hours in the oven

**boneless pork shoulder or leg** 2kg, skin removed, rolled and tied
**fennel seeds** 2 tbsp
**chilli flakes** 1 tsp
**dried oregano** 1 tbsp
**rosemary leaves** chopped, 2 tbsp
**olive oil**

ROAST GARLIC MASH
**whole garlic bulbs** 3, tops sliced off
**olive oil**
**potatoes** 1.5kg, peeled and cut into chunks
**butter** 150g
**crème fraîche** 200g

■ Heat the oven to 190°C/fan 170°C/gas 5. Put the garlic for the mash on a large sheet of foil, drizzle with 2 tbsp oil and season. Seal the foil and roast for 50 minutes then remove. Turn down the oven to 140°C/fan 120°C/gas 1.

■ Season the pork well then fry on all sides in a large frying pan until browned. Mix together the spices and herbs. Rub 2 tbsp oil over the pork, then roll in the herb and spice mix. Put on a roasting rack in a roasting tin and roast for 4 hours.

■ To make the mash, simmer the potatoes in salted water until tender – about 20 minutes. Drain, add the butter and mash well. Add the crème fraîche and season. Squeeze the garlic out of its skin into the mash and mix. Serve with the pork. **Serves 6**

It's worth spending a few extra pounds on organic pork or pork from a specific breed (such as Tamworth) for this, as it will have a much better texture and flavour.

# Swiss chard and olive tart

30 minutes + 25 minutes in the oven

**ready-roll shortcrust pastry** 350g
**Swiss chard** 250g
**butter**
**spring onions** 4, finely sliced
**ricotta cheese** 250g
**eggs** 2, beaten
**Parmesan cheese** grated, 6 tbsp
**green or black olives** 12, pitted and
    halved

■ Heat the oven to 200°C/fan 180°C/gas 6. Line a 22cm tart tin with the pastry and blind bake for 15–20 minutes. Turn the temperature down to 180°C/fan 160°C/gas 4. Meanwhile, separate the leaves and stems from the chard, chop the stems into dice and shred the leaves. Blanch both in boiling water, but one at a time; the stems will need about 3 minutes and the leaves 1 minute. Drain and squeeze dry.

■ Melt some butter in a pan and fry the spring onions for a minute until soft, add the chard and season well. Cook until any liquid has evaporated. Tip into a bowl and stir in the ricotta, beaten eggs, half of the Parmesan and the olives. Pour into the pastry case and sprinkle the rest of the Parmesan on top. Bake for about 25 minutes until firm to the touch. Brown the top under a hot grill if it needs it. **Serves 4**

Sort of spinachy but with a stronger flavour, Swiss chard leaves are best cooked separately to the stalks as they take less time.

# Slow-cooked lamb with vegetables

15 minutes + 5 hours in the oven

**onions** 5, cut into thick slices

**carrots** 500g, cut into chunks

**garlic** 2 whole heads, separated into cloves

**thyme and rosemary** a large handful of each

**leg of lamb** about 2.5kg

**dry white wine** 1 bottle (750ml)

**potatoes** 1 kg, thickly sliced

**butternut squash** 1, peeled and chopped into chunks

**cherry tomatoes** 500g

■ Heat the oven to 200°C/fan 180°C/gas 6. Scatter the onion, carrot, garlic and herbs over the bottom of a large roasting dish. Lay the lamb on top. Roast for 30 minutes. Pour in the wine, season well and cover with foil.

■ Reduce the oven temperature to 180°C/fan 160°C/gas 4 and cook for 3½ hours, checking occasionally and basting with the wine. Remove the foil, add the potatoes, squash and tomatoes, and cook for 1 hour or until the potatoes are soft and the meat is falling off the bone.

**Serves 6**

You could also use lamb shoulder for this recipe.

# Peas and spring cabbage with pancetta

25 minutes

**peas** 300g (you'll need about 600g peas in the pod for this)
**butter**
**pancetta or streaky bacon** 350g, chopped
**spring cabbage** 1 head, tough outer leaves discarded, then finely sliced
**nutmeg** freshly grated, to season

■ Cook the peas in boiling water until just tender, drain and cool under running water. Melt a knob of butter in a large pan and add the pancetta or bacon. Cook for a couple of minutes, then stir in the cabbage. Cover and cook on a low heat for 10–15 minutes or until just tender. Add the peas and heat through. Season with salt, lots of pepper and grated nutmeg. **Serves 6**

If peas in pod aren't quite in season then frozen ones will do nicely instead.

# Asparagus with almonds, capers and browned butter

10 minutes

asparagus 1 bunch, about 250g, ends
    trimmed
butter 50g
flaked almonds a large handful
capers (those packed in salt are best)
    2 tbsp, rinsed and squeezed dry

■ Half fill a frying pan with water and bring it to the boil. Add the asparagus and simmer for 3–5 minutes or until tender. Lift a spear out and see if it is slightly droopy when you hold it by the thick end – that's the sign that it's ready. Drain.

■ Meanwhile, heat the butter in the frying pan and add the almonds and capers. Toss until the almonds are browned and the capers are frizzled; the butter should have browned as well. Tip over the asparagus and season with black pepper (if you used salted capers you won't need any more salt). **Serves 2**

Asparagus is in season in Britain between April and June, and is worth eating as much as possible while it is around.

# Jerseys in a bag

**5 minutes + 25–35 minutes in the oven**

**Jersey Royal potatoes** 500g, washed and
dried well
**bulb spring onions** 12, stalks trimmed
short
**lemon** 1, zested and halved
**butter** 50g

■ Heat the oven to 200°C/fan 180°C/gas 6.
Divide the potatoes and onions into
4 piles. Put each portion into a
parchment baking bag (sometimes called
multi-purpose cooking bags) with some
of the lemon zest, a squeeze of juice
(from the lemon halves) and a quarter of
the butter.

■ Put on a baking sheet and cook for
25–35 minutes, depending on the size of
the potatoes. Check the potatoes in 1 bag
with the point of a knife to see if they are
cooked. Serve in the bags. **Serves 4 as a
side dish.**

Start-of-season Jersey Royals are
miniscule in size and can be left whole.
Halve or quarter the bigger ones.

# Orange, vodka and sweet basil sherbet

**45 minutes plus freezing time**

oranges 4 large
caster sugar 8 tbsp
low-fat bio yoghurt 500g carton
vodka 4 tbsp
basil about 10 large leaves
banana 1, chopped

You can leave out the vodka, but this will set the sherbet hard, so it will need to soften in the fridge for half an hour before serving.

■ Slice off the tops of the oranges about a quarter of the way down; grate the zest from the four lids. Scoop the insides into a bowl. Cut a thin sliver off the base of the orange shells so that they stand steady, then put them in the freezer.

■ Press the orange flesh through a sieve and use a ladle to squeeze out as much juice as possible. Pour the juice into a pan and add the zest from the orange lids. Boil the juice and zest until reduced to about 125ml. Stir in the sugar and allow to cool a little. Stir in the yoghurt and vodka, pour into a freezer box, and freeze until solid. Tip into a food processor and add the basil and chopped banana. Whiz until smooth. Freeze until it holds its shape and then scoop into the orange shells to serve. **Serves 4**

# Tangerine posset

30 minutes + chilling

**double cream** 568ml carton
**tangerines** 3, zested in strips and juiced
**golden caster sugar** 3 tbsp
**lemon** 1, juiced

■ Put the cream in a pan with the tangerine zest and bring to a simmer. Turn off the heat and leave to infuse for 20 minutes.

■ Fish out the zest and bring the cream back up to just below boiling. Stir in the sugar and then the juices. The mixture will start to thicken so pour it straight into 6 small glasses or pots. Cool slightly then chill until set, about 3 hours.

**Serves 6**

The acidity in the fruit causes the cream to thicken so make sure you have a good sharp lemon for this.

# Mango and passionfruit fool

**20 minutes + chilling**

**mangoes** 2 ripe, peeled
**lime** ½, juiced
**0% fat Greek yoghurt** 500g
**passion fruits** 2

■ Chop the mango into dice and divide almost half of it among 4 small bowls or glasses, saving some for the topping.

■ Put the remaining mango in a blender or mini food processor with the lime juice, and whiz to a purée. Beat the yoghurt until smooth then swirl in the mango purée.

■ Pour into bowls, scatter with the remaining diced mango and scoop the seeds of half a passionfruit on to each one. Chill until thick. **Serves 4**

For a creamier texture use full-fat Greek yoghurt.

# Papaya with chilli caramel

15 minutes

light muscovado sugar 4 tbsp
red chilli 1 small, seeded, cut into thin
   strips
lime 1, zest in strips and juice
papaya 1 ripe, skin removed

■ Put the sugar, chilli and 100ml water in a pan and bring to the boil. Simmer for 5 minutes to make a light syrup. Stir in the lime zest and juice, pour into a jug and cool.
■ Cut the papaya into thin wedges and arrange on 2 plates. Pour over the syrup and serve. **Serves 2**

Tropical fruit adds a brightness to a season when no British fruit grows. You can also use this syrup with pineapple and mango.

# Rhubarb slumps

**40 minutes**

---

**rhubarb** 400g, cut into chunks
**light muscovado sugar** 6 tbsp
**orange** 1, zest and half-juiced
**oats** 100g
**double cream** 6 tbsp
**dark muscovado sugar** 2 tbsp

■ Heat the oven to 180°C/fan 160°C/gas 4. Mix the rhubarb with the light muscovado sugar, orange zest and half of the juice and spoon into 1 large (or 4 small) dishes. Mix the oats with the cream and dark muscovado, and drop spoonfuls of the mixture all over the surface of the rhubarb.

■ Bake for 30 minutes until the topping is browned, and the rhubarb has bubbled up around it. **Serves 4**

Forced rhubarb grows in dark sheds between December and March. It's a gentler pink than summer rhubarb.

# Grilled lettuce with Camembert and raspberry vinegar

10 minutes

**little gem lettuces** 4, **or cos hearts** 2
**olive oil**
**crusty bread** 4 slices, toasted
**Camembert cheese** ½ of one, sliced thickly
**raspberry vinegar** to serve

■ Cut the little gem lettuces in half, or the cos into quarters, through the stem, making sure the leaves hold together. Sprinkle with a little olive oil and season with salt flakes and freshly milled black pepper.

■ Put the lettuce, cut-side down, on a baking sheet and grill for 3–5 minutes, turning once, until the stems are just becoming tender. Divide among the toast slices, lay the cheese on top and grill until the cheese starts to bubble. Spoon over some raspberry vinegar and serve hot.

**Serves 4**

Firm, juicy lettuces such as little gem or cos work particularly well for this recipe, but iceberg would be too juicy.

# Courgettes with sun-dried pangritata

25 minutes

**fresh breadcrumbs** a handful
**lemon thyme leaves** 1 tbsp
**sun-dried tomatoes** 50g
**pine nuts** 2 tbsp
**extra-virgin olive oil**
**small courgettes** 16, halved lengthways

■ Heat the oven to 200°C/fan 180°C/gas 6. Whiz the breadcrumbs with the lemon thyme and sun-dried tomatoes in a food processor. Mix the nuts and 1 tbsp oil with the crumb mix, season and spread on a baking sheet.

■ Put the courgettes and 1 tbsp oil into a roasting tin. Bake both for about 12 minutes or until the courgettes are tender and the pangritata golden and crunchy (take it out if it browns too much before the courgettes are done). Sprinkle the pangritata over the courgettes.

**Serves 4**

New season courgettes should be nice and small, about the length of your finger.

# Prawn cocktail

30 minutes

**iceberg lettuce** 1, quartered and finely shredded
**king prawns** 250g, cooked and peeled
**cayenne pepper** to finish
**lime** to serve

MARIE ROSE SAUCE
**egg yolk** 1, very fresh, preferably organic
**Dijon mustard** 1 tsp
**lemon juice** 1 tsp
**sunflower oil** 200ml
**double cream** 2 tbsp
**tomato ketchup** 2 tbsp
**Worcestershire sauce** 1 tsp
**Tabasco sauce** a few dashes

■ To make the sauce, put the egg yolk, mustard and lemon juice in a mixing bowl, and whisk together using a hand or electric whisk. Slowly start to add the oil as you whisk – you want the finished consistency to be pretty thick. Mix in the cream, tomato ketchup, Worcestershire sauce and Tabasco.

■ Fill 6 glasses about halfway up with the lettuce, then fill to the top with prawns. Spoon the sauce over the prawns, sprinkle with cayenne and add a wedge of lime. **Serves 6**

King prawns look more dramatic than smaller North Atlantic prawns but both have an equally good flavour.

# Warm broad bean and lentil salad

30 minutes

**Puy lentils** 250g
**red onion** 1 small, sliced
**broad beans** 300g (about 1kg of pods
    should give you this weight of beans)
**olive oil**
**red wine vinegar** 1 tbsp
**mint** 1 bunch, chopped
**soft goat's cheese** 150g

■ Put the lentils in a saucepan with the onion, cover with water, bring to the boil and simmer for 20 minutes until tender – the water should be absorbed. Season well.

■ Meanwhile, cook the broad beans in simmering water for 5 minutes until just tender. Drain, then tip back into the pan, add 2 tbsp olive oil and warm for 2 minutes. Add to the lentils with the red wine vinegar and mint, and season well. Taste and add more seasoning or vinegar if you like. Add the goat's cheese in blobs and fold it in carefully. **Serves 4**

Broad beans are wonderful when they are young and tender. No need to waste time double podding at this point in the season.

# Tomato tart

1 hour 50 minutes + 1 hour cooling

PASTRY
**plain flour** 200g
**butter** 100g
**Parmesan cheese** 100g, freshly grated
**egg** 1, beaten

FILLING
**cherry tomatoes** 3 × 400g packs
**red chilli** 1, finely chopped
**garlic** 2 cloves, finely chopped
**thyme sprigs** 4, leaves stripped
**olive oil** 3 tbsp
**Dijon mustard** 3 tbsp

Roasting tomatoes intensifies their flavour, and this trick works with all tomatoes.

■ Heat the oven to 160°C/fan 140°C/gas 3. Spread the tomatoes over a large baking sheet lined with baking parchment and roast for 30 minutes.

■ In a bowl, rub together the flour and butter or pulse in a food processor until they resemble breadcrumbs, then stir in the grated Parmesan. Add the egg and mix until it forms a ball – you may need to add a tiny splash of water. Turn out on to a lightly floured surface and knead briefly. Roll out the pastry, line a 25cm springform tin and freeze for 30 minutes.

■ Turn up the oven to 180°C/fan 160°C/gas 4. Mix the chilli, garlic and thyme leaves in a bowl with 3 tbsp oil and roasted tomatoes, then season. Spread the pastry base with the mustard, then fill with the tomatoes. Bake for 30 minutes, then reduce the heat to 160°C/fan 140°C/gas 3 and cook for a further 40 minutes. When cooked, turn the oven off but leave the tart in the cooling oven for 1 hour. **Serves 6**

# Welsh lamb with honeyed carrots

**40 minutes**

olive oil
**Welsh lamb chops** 4
**clear honey** 1 tbsp
**wholegrain mustard** 1 tbsp
**carrots** ½ bunch, about 250g, trimmed
    and halved
**lemon** 1, halved

■ Heat the oven to 200°C/fan 180°C/gas 6. Oil the lamb chops and season them with salt flakes and freshly milled black pepper. Mix 1 tbsp olive oil with the honey and mustard in a large bowl and use this mixture to coat the carrots.

■ Arrange the carrots on a baking sheet and cook for 15 minutes. Add the chops on top of the carrots and cook for a further 15–20 minutes until the fat is cooked through and tinged brown. Serve with lemon halves to squeeze over.

**Serves 2**

The start of the summer is the time to eat sweet, new season Welsh lamb. Treat it simply with just a minimum of seasoning so that you can appreciate its flavour.

# Stuffed peppers with rice, pine nuts and dill

50 minutes

**olive oil**

**onion** 1, finely chopped

**pine nuts** 4 tbsp

**smoked paprika** 1 tsp

**ground cinnamon** 1 tsp

**basmati rice** 125g, cooked

**dill** 4 tbsp, chopped

**feta cheese** 75–100g, cubed

**peppers** 2 orange, red or yellow, halved and seeds removed

■ Heat the oven to 180°C/fan 160°C/gas 4. Heat 2 tbsp olive oil in a frying pan and cook the onion over a low heat until golden. Add the pine nuts and brown lightly. Stir in the spices and cook for a minute. Add the rice and dill and stir together. Season well. Fold in the feta.

■ Put the peppers, cut-side up, in a shallow baking dish or roasting tin. Divide the mixture among them and drizzle liberally with olive oil. Cover with foil and roast for 40 minutes until the peppers are tender, then remove the foil and cook for a further 5 minutes. **Serves 2**

Home-grown peppers tend to be sweeter than imports so make the most of them in season.

# Sesame-crusted tuna

20 minutes + 1 hour resting time

**mixed black and white sesame seeds**
100g (or toast half of the white seeds
to a light brown colour)
**tuna loin** 500g, cut into thick logs
**cucumber** 1, cut into matchsticks
**spring onions** 1 bunch, cut into
matchsticks
**coriander** 1 bunch, roughly chopped
**kaffir lime leaf** 1, thinly sliced (optional)
**lime** 1, juiced
**green or red chilli** 1, seeds removed, finely
diced

DRESSING
**wasabi paste** ½ tsp
**rice wine vinegar** 3 tbsp
**mirin** 100ml
**soy sauce** 100ml
**sesame oil** 1 tbsp

■ Mix the sesame seeds with some seasoning and spread on a flat plate. Firmly roll the tuna in the mix to coat the outside with seeds. Heat a non-stick pan over a high heat until very hot, then sear the tuna on each side for 20 seconds: you only want it to cook a little way through. Remove from the pan and leave to rest for 1 hour – this allows the fish to firm up and makes slicing easier.

■ Toss all the salad ingredients together. For the dressing, mix the wasabi and rice vinegar until blended, then stir in the mirin, soy sauce and sesame oil. Use a sharp knife to slice the tuna into 5mm slices. Arrange on a plate, top with a handful of the tossed salad and drizzle over some dressing. **Serves 6**

Make sure your knife is very sharp before slicing the tuna – and don't use a serrated knife.

# Oven-roasted ratatouille with garlic bread

1 hour

**olive oil**

**red onions** 2, cut into wedges, leaving the
    root end on

**peppers** 7, a mix of orange and red,
    quartered and seeds removed

**aubergines** 2 medium, cut into quarters

**plum tomatoes** 4, cut into quarters

**baby courgettes** 8, trimmed and halved

**garlic** 2 cloves, crushed

**thyme** 4 sprigs

**sugocasa, passata or tomato juice** 400ml

GARLIC BREAD

**baguette** 1 small

**garlic cloves** 2, crushed

**butter** 100g, at room temperature

■ Heat the oven to 180°C/fan 160°C/gas 4. Pour 3 tbsp olive oil into a large roasting tin. Add the onions, peppers, aubergines and tomatoes to the tin and toss well to coat in the olive oil. Roast for 30 minutes. Add the courgettes, garlic and thyme to the ratatouille with the sugocasa, passata or tomato juice and some seasoning, mix well and return to the oven to cook for a further 20 minutes.

■ Meanwhile, cut the baguette in half lengthways, mix the garlic with the butter and spread over the baguette. Toast under a heated grill until golden. Slice and serve with the ratatouille.

**Serves 4**

The deeper the tin you use, the more juice the veg will retain as it cooks.

# Summer prawn and fish pie

## 50 minutes

**white fish fillets** 750g skinless
**fish stock or water** 300ml
**peeled prawns** 100g
**peas** 100g fresh or frozen (if fresh then
    cook for 3 minutes)
**lemon** 1, zest and juice
**butter** 40g
**plain flour** 1 tbsp
**dill** 1 bunch, fronds chopped
**ready-roll filo pastry** 8 sheets (about
    100g)

■ Heat the oven to 200°C/fan 180°C/gas 6. Put the fish in a frying pan with the stock and bring to a simmer, then cook for 3 minutes until the fish is opaque. Drain the stock into a jug. Flake the fish into a bowl and add the prawns and peas. Add the lemon zest and juice to taste to the stock. Melt the butter in a saucepan and stir in the flour to make a roux (smooth paste). Add the stock little by little, stirring constantly until you have a sauce. Season well and stir in the dill, fish, peas and prawns.

■ Tip this into a baking dish. Cover the surface with filo pastry, scrunching up each sheet so it looks like a loosely crumpled ball. Melt the rest of the butter and brush it all over the pastry. Bake for 20–25 minutes until the pastry is golden.
**Serves 4**

Lighten pie recipes in summer by using crisp filo as a topping.

# Sort-of moussaka

1 hour

---

**lamb mince** 450g

**onions** 2, finely chopped

**garlic** 2 cloves, crushed

**chopped tomatoes** 1 × 400g tin

**white wine** 1 glass

**ground cinnamon** 1 tsp

**aubergines** 3 young, firm ones, cut into
1cm slices

**olive oil**

**eggs** 2

**ready-made fresh cheese sauce or
béchamel** 1 × 300ml

**bay leaves** 4 small ones, fresh or dried

■ Heat the oven to 200°C/fan 180°C/gas 6. Heat a heavy frying pan and add the mince. Brown it well, breaking up any lumps, then lift it out of the oil it will have created, add the onions and garlic to the pan and cook until soft. Return the mince to the pan along with the tomato, white wine, cinnamon and some salt and pepper. Cook over a low heat for 30 minutes. Meanwhile, brush the aubergine slices with oil and lay them on a baking sheet. Cook in the oven for 20 minutes until browned and soft.

■ Beat the eggs into the cheese or béchamel sauce. Divide half the meat among each of 4 baking dishes, then add half the aubergine. Top with the remaining meat, then the remaining aubergine. Finish with the sauce, put a bay leaf on each and bake for 20 minutes, until browned. **Serves 4**

Young aubergines don't need salting but older ones would benefit from it.

# Baked trout with white wine and fennel

50 minutes

**fennel bulb** 1 large, finely sliced
**whole trout** 2, gutted and cleaned
**tarragon** a small bunch, chopped
**shallots** 2, finely sliced
**lemon** 1, thinly sliced
**small button mushrooms** 2 handfuls, halved
**butter** 50g
**dry white wine** a couple of splashes

■ Heat the oven to 200°C/fan 180°C/gas 6. Make a bed of fennel in the middle of two large rectangles of baking paper. Sit the fish on top, then stuff them with the rest of the fennel, half the tarragon and the shallots.

■ Top each fish with the lemon slices and scatter over the mushrooms and remaining tarragon. Dot with butter and pour over the wine. Fold the paper around each fish to enclose, put on a baking sheet and bake for 30 minutes. Serve in the parcels, to be opened at the table. **Serves 2**

Make sure trout is nice and fresh – firm-fleshed, bright-eyed and red around the gills.

# Chicken with saffron and chilli

30 minutes + marinating

**saffron threads** a pinch
**red chilli** 1, seeded and finely chopped
**mint** chopped, 2 tbsp
**garlic** 2 cloves, crushed
**olive oil**
**lemon** 1, juiced and skin cut into chunks
**chicken breasts** 4, skin on
**couscous** 250g
**peas** 150g, fresh or frozen
**cherry tomatoes** 200g, halved

Chillies vary in strength. If you want a hot one then choose a tiny Thai bird's-eye chilli.

■ Put the saffron, chilli, mint, garlic, 3 tbsp oil, half the lemon juice and the lemon skin pieces with the chicken in a plastic bag or bowl. Mix thoroughly and marinate in the fridge for at least 20 minutes.

■ Heat the grill to medium high. Put the chicken, skin-side up, on a roasting tray with the marinade. Sprinkle salt over the skin and grill until the skin is crisp and golden – about 7–10 minutes. Turn over and cook for a further 5–6 minutes or until the chicken is cooked through. Meanwhile, put the couscous in a bowl, pour over 400ml boiling water, cover and leave until all the water has been absorbed.

■ Cook the peas in a pan of boiling water for 3 minutes, drain and mix into the couscous along with the tomato, the rest of the lemon juice and lots of seasoning. Serve with the chicken, lemon chunks and any juices. **Serves 4**

# Mediterranean vegetable tian

40 minutes

**thyme or lemon thyme** 1 tbsp leaves, chopped
**balsamic vinegar** 1 tbsp
**olive oil**
**red pepper** 2, seeds removed and cut into strips
**courgettes** 3, sliced on an angle
**red onion** 1, sliced into half moons
**beef tomatoes** 2, halved and sliced
**Parmesan cheese** a small lump, grated

■ Heat the oven to 180°C/fan 160°C/gas 4. Mix the thyme leaves with the vinegar and 2 tbsp olive oil. Season well. Layer the vegetables in 4 individual baking dishes or tians (the earthenware type), coating them with the thyme mixture as you go and propping them up against the sides so you can see them all. Sprinkle over the Parmesan and bake for 30 minutes. Serve with bread and salad. **Serves 4**

If you are using ordinary thyme, add a squeeze of lemon to bump up the flavour.

# Runner beans with tomato and oregano

40 minutes

---

**runner beans** 450g
**olive oil**
**onion** 1, finely sliced
**garlic** 2 cloves, finely sliced
**turmeric** 2 tsp
**kalonji** (black onion seeds) 2 tsp
**oregano** 2 sprigs
**cherry or plum tomatoes** 2 × 400g tins

■ Snap off the ends of the beans and pull off any strings from the outside edges. Slice the beans diagonally.

■ Heat a good slug of oil in a deep frying pan, add the onion and garlic and cook over a low heat for about 4 minutes until tender but not browned. Add the spices and stir. Add the oregano and tomatoes and bring to the boil. Add the beans, cover and reduce heat to a simmer. Cook for 30 minutes or until the beans are tender – they won't be bright green by now. Season well. **Serves 6**

You can find kalonji seeds in major supermarkets and Indian shops; they are also called nigella seeds.

# Tabbouleh

30 minutes + 30 minutes standing

**bulgar (cracked wheat)** 30g
**firm ripe tomatoes** 600g, finely diced
**spring onions** ½ bunch, trimmed and very
    thinly sliced
**flat-leaf parsley** 2 bunches, finely
    chopped
**mint** ½ bunch, leaves only, finely chopped
**ground cinnamon** ¼ tsp
**Lebanese 7-spice mixture** ½ tsp
**finely ground black pepper** ¼ tsp
**lemon** 1, squeezed
**extra virgin olive oil** 150ml
**little gem lettuces** 4, to serve

■ Rinse the bulgar in 2 to 3 changes of cold water, drain well and put in a salad bowl large enough to take the finished dish. Add the tomatoes, spring onions, parsley and mint to the bowl. Cover with a tea towel and leave for about 30 minutes for the bulghar to soften.

■ Add the spices and season to taste. Add the lemon juice and olive oil and toss everything together. Taste and adjust the seasoning again if necessary.

**Serves 4**

You'll find 7-spice mixture in Middle Eastern shops, but if you can't get hold of any, use ground all-spice instead.

# Gooseberries poached with vanilla and elderflower

15 minutes

gooseberries 500g, topped and tailed

caster sugar 100g

elderflower cordial 3 tbsp

vanilla pod 1, split along its length

Madeira cake 4 slices

crème fraîche, cream or ice cream
    to serve

■ Tip the gooseberries into a large frying pan and add the sugar, cordial and vanilla pod. Heat gently over a low heat until the gooseberries start to get juicy, then shake the pan and leave to cook with a lid on for 8 minutes.

■ Take the lid off and cook for a further 2 minutes to reduce the liquid. Serve over slices of Madeira cake with a slug of crème fraîche, cream or spooned over ice cream. **Serves 4**

Pairing gooseberries with elderflower brings out their gooseberry personality and takes the edge off their tartness.

# Raspberry and chocolate brownie muffins

30 minutes

**dark chocolate** (70% cocoa solids) 100g

**butter** 100g

**eggs** 2, beaten

**golden caster sugar** 230g

**self-raising flour** 100g

**raspberries** 150g

**icing sugar** for dusting

■ Heat the oven to 180°C/fan 160°C/gas 4. Melt the chocolate and butter in a saucepan over a low heat and mix together. Remove from the heat and beat in the eggs, sugar and flour. Add the raspberries and mix gently.

■ Pour into the muffin cases and bake for 20–25 minutes. Cool slightly and then gently take them out of the tin. Lightly dust the tops with icing sugar. **Makes 8**

These are quite delicate, so use a flexible 8-hole muffin tin (the rubbery ones), or line a rigid tin with paper cases.

# Pimm's and strawberry jellies with orange cream

20 minutes + setting time

**leaf gelatine** 3 sheets
**lemonade** 400ml
**Pimm's No. 1 Cup** 175ml
**lemon** ½, juiced
**lime** ½, juiced
**double cream** 284ml carton
**caster sugar** 2 tbsp
**oranges** 3, 2 peeled and segmented with a sharp knife, 1 zested
**strawberries** 250g, hulled
**mint sprigs** to decorate

■ Soak the gelatine in cold water until soft (it will take about 2 minutes). Heat half the lemonade until just about boiling and remove from the heat. Lift the gelatine out of the water and stir into the warm lemonade until dissolved. Add the Pimm's, lemon and lime juice, and remaining lemonade. Pour through a sieve into a bowl and refrigerate until set.

■ Lightly whip the cream and stir in the sugar and orange zest. Slice the strawberries and stir half of them through the set jelly. To serve, dollop some jelly in a glass then add more strawberries and some orange segments. Finish with a blob of the orange cream, a sprig of mint and, if you like, a strip of zest. **Serves 6**

If you can't get leaf gelatine, use powdered gelatine instead, following the packet instructions.

# Apricot galettes

55 minutes

ready-roll puff pastry 375g packet
marzipan ½ packet (about 100g)
apricots 6 very ripe ones, halved and
    pitted
light muscovado sugar to sprinkle
apricot jam to glaze

Look out for puff pastry made with
butter as it tastes better, or brush
ordinary puff pastry with melted butter
before cooking.

■ Heat the oven to 200°C/fan 180°C/gas 6
and put a baking sheet in the oven. Cut
4 circles out of the pastry using a saucer
as a template. Using a sharp knife score
a line about 1cm from the edge. Roll out
the marzipan to the thickness of a £1 coin
and cut out 4 circles to fit inside the
scored lines.

■ Put the pastry on a second baking
sheet, place a circle of marzipan in the
middle of each and arrange 3 apricot
halves, cut-side up, on each. Sprinkle a
little sugar into each apricot. Put the
baking sheet into the oven on top of the
hot baking sheet – this will help crisp the
base. Cook for 20–25 minutes until the
pastry is puffed and browned and the
apricots are slightly caramelised around
the edges. While they're still hot, brush
with apricot jam to glaze. **Makes 4**

# Peach pavlova

30 minutes + 1 ½ hours cooking +
2 hours cooling time

**egg whites** 4
**unrefined caster sugar** 250g
**peaches or nectarines** 8, stoned and
    sliced
**double cream** 284ml carton
**crème fraîche** 100ml
**honey** to drizzle
**golden caster sugar** 2 tbsp, for sprinkling

■ Heat the oven to 140°C/fan 120°C/gas 1.
Line a baking sheet with baking
parchment. Put an 18cm plate in the
middle of the parchment and draw
around it to make a template for your
pavlova.

■ Use an electric mixer to whisk the egg
whites until stiff (about 3 minutes). Add
the caster sugar and whisk until evenly
blended. The mixture should be very stiff
and shiny. Use a blob of meringue to
stick the parchment to the baking sheet.
Spoon ½ the meringue across the marked
circle to make the base, then heap the
rest around the edges to make a nest
shape. Bake in the middle of the oven for
1 ½ hours, then turn off the heat and
leave the meringue until the oven is cool.

■ Halve the peaches, remove the stones
and cut into wedges. Whisk the cream
until it just holds in soft folds. Carefully
mix in the crème fraîche, then spoon into
the pavlova. Arrange peaches on top then
drizzle with honey and a sprinkling of
golden caster sugar. **Serves 6**

For the perfect meringue, whisk it stiff
and cook it long and slow, and remember
not to use eggs straight from the fridge.

# Raspberry and rosewater fool

15 minutes

**fresh or frozen raspberries** 300g
**rosewater** 2 tsp
**caster sugar** 100g
**virtually fat-free quark** 250g carton
**Greek yoghurt** 200g carton

■ Keep back a good handful of raspberries, then tip the rest into a food processor with the rosewater and ¾ of the sugar. Blitz until smooth, then sieve into a bowl.

■ In a separate bowl, beat the quark with the remaining sugar, then beat in the yoghurt, then the raspberry purée. Spoon into 4 glasses and scatter the remaining raspberries over the top. Serve immediately or chill for up to 8 hours.

**Serves 4**

Rosewater can be bought in some supermarkets and in chemists. The stuff in chemists is stronger, so make sure it's edible.

# Summer puddings

30 minutes + overnight chilling

---

**red, white and black currants** 1 punnet of
each
**raspberries** 2 punnets
**golden caster sugar** 2 tbsp
**white bread** 12 slices of a good quality
variety, thinly sliced and crusts
removed

■ Tip the fruit into a saucepan. Add the
sugar plus 6 tbsp water and bring to a
gentle simmer. Cook for a couple of
minutes until the fruit just begins to
burst and gives off lots of juice, then
cool. Add more sugar if you like.

■ Cut 6 circles from the bread to fit the
base of 6 small pudding basins or
moulds; keep the trimmings. Cut the rest
of the bread into fingers. Line the basins
with the bread, trimming the fingers to
fit. Fill with most of the fruit and juice.
Use the rest of the bread to cover the
tops of the puddings. Put the puddings
on a tray, with another tray and tins on
top to weigh it down. Chill overnight.

■ Turn the puddings out. If the juice
hasn't soaked through completely, brush
the outside of the bread with a little
more. Serve with cream and the left-over
fruit. **Serves 6**

If you can't find white currants then
double the amount of red.

# Baked vanilla peaches

50 minutes

peaches 4
butter 50g
vanilla pod 1
honey 4 tbsp
white wine 300ml (whatever you have to hand is fine)
ice cream or crème fraîche to serve

■ Heat the oven to 160°C/fan 140°C/gas 3. Cut a cross in the bottom of each peach (the end without the stalk). Rub a roasting tin or baking dish with the butter and add the peaches. Cut the vanilla pod in half and scrape out the seeds and add to the peach dish along with the broken pod. Top each peach with a spoonful of honey, add the white wine and bake for 45 minutes. Serve with ice cream or crème fraîche. **Serves 4**

Subjecting peaches to heat brings out their sweetness and makes them somehow even peachier. These can be served hot or cold and will keep for a day in the fridge.

# Strawberry tart

50 minutes + chilling

ready-roll sweet pastry 500g
mascarpone or clotted cream 100g
strawberry jelly ½ packet
small strawberries or halved large ones
    500g, hulled

Organic strawberries are often more fully
flavoured than mass-produced varieties
such as Elsanta

■ Heat the oven to 190°C/fan 170°C/gas 5. Lightly butter a 24cm tart tin. Roll out the pastry (use a bit of flour to stop it sticking) and use to line the tart tin, then chill for 25 minutes. Line the base of the pastry with baking paper and beans and bake for 15 minutes. Reduce the heat to 150°C/fan 130°C/gas 2 and bake for a further 10 minutes, then remove the baking paper and beans and cook for 10 minutes more.

■ Leave the pastry to cool a little, then remove from the tin and transfer to a serving plate. When it's totally cold, spread the mascarpone or clotted cream over the pastry base. Melt the jelly crystals in 175ml hot water, cool and, when it starts to thicken, add the strawberries and carefully mix to coat them. Put the strawberries upright in a single layer in the case and spoon in enough of the remaining jelly to cover them. **Serves 6**

# Berry fool

**10 minutes + chilling**

**mixed berries** 500g
**icing sugar** 2 tbsp
**lemons** 2, zested
**whipping cream** 568ml carton

■ Blitz the berries and icing sugar in a food processor, then sieve and add the lemon zest. Whip the cream in a separate bowl until thick and fold in the fruit purée. Spoon into glasses and chill for 1 hour before serving. **Serves 6**

Use whatever berries are at their best for this, or even a single variety.

# Grilled fig and Parma ham tart

10 minutes + 30 minutes in the oven

---

**ready-roll puff pastry** 1 pack, about 350g

**mascarpone** 4 tbsp

**Parma ham** 8–12 slices

**figs** 8–12, depending on how big they are, halved

**dark muscovado sugar** 2 tbsp

**olive oil**

**egg yolk** 1, beaten

■ Heat the oven to 180°C/fan 160°C/gas 4 and put a baking sheet in the oven to heat up. Lay the pastry out on a separate, oiled baking sheet and trim the edges straight. Score a 1cm border around the edge. Spread the mascarpone within the scored line and then arrange the Parma ham on top. Arrange the figs on top of the ham in rows, cut-side up. Mix the sugar with enough oil to make a runny paste and brush this over the figs.

■ Season the tart well with flakes of salt and freshly milled black pepper. Brush the pastry with the egg yolk. Bake on top of the hot baking sheet for 30 minutes or until the pastry has puffed and browned and the figs are caramelised around the edges. **Serves 4**

Figs should be slightly yielding to the touch which shows they are ripe.

# Garlicky mushrooms on toast

15 minutes

**butter** 50g
**field mushrooms** 4 medium-size,
    quartered
**garlic** 1 large clove, chopped
**thyme** 1 tbsp, chopped
**baby button mushrooms** 100g
**chestnut mushrooms** 100g, halved
**crusty bread or sourdough** 2 thick slices
**flat-leaf parsley** 1 tbsp, chopped

■ Melt half the butter in a large frying pan and add the field mushrooms. Cook over a gentle heat for 3–4 minutes or until the mushrooms begin to soften and become juicy. Add the remaining butter, the garlic, thyme and the other mushrooms to the pan. Season and continue to cook for 5 minutes. The mushrooms should become really juicy and tender – add more butter to the pan if necessary.

■ Meanwhile, toast the bread and put 1 slice on each plate. Toss the parsley into the mushrooms and pile on to the toast.

**Serves 2**

In season you could use half field mushrooms and half wild mushrooms.

# Pumpkin soup with chilli and sour cream

**40 minutes**

pumpkin 1 kg, peeled and chopped

olive oil

red chillies 1–2, seeded and finely
   chopped

garlic 1 clove

milk 375ml

chicken or vegetable stock powder, cubes
   or fresh, made up to 750ml

coriander a handful, roughly chopped
   (optional)

sour cream to serve

■ Heat the oven to 200°C/fan 180°C/gas 6.
Put the pumpkin in a roasting tin, drizzle
with 4 tbsp oil and roast for 15–20
minutes, until tender and a little browned
around the edges.

■ Tip the pumpkin, chilli and garlic into
a saucepan with the milk and stock and
bring to the boil (don't worry if it splits).
Reduce the heat and simmer for
8 minutes. Cool a little then whiz in a
blender until smooth and season well.
Stir through the coriander, if using, and
top each bowl with a dollop of sour
cream. **Serves 4**

Use classic pumpkin, blue-skinned
Crown Prince, or butternut squash for
this recipe.

# Swede and bacon cakes with dill sauce

50 minutes + 1 hour chilling

**swede** 1 (about 800g), peeled and cut into small chunks

**potatoes** 2 (about 400g), peeled and cut into chunks

**onion** 1, finely chopped

**oil** for frying

**lardons or chopped bacon** 200g

**flat-leaf parsley** chopped, 2 tbsp

**flour** for coating

**butter** 25g

**dill** chopped, 2 tbsp

**crème fraîche** 200ml

**green salad** to serve

■ Cook the swede and potatoes in boiling, salted water for 15–20 minutes until tender. Drain well and mash together. Fry the onion in a little oil, then add the lardons and fry until lightly browned. Add to the mash with the parsley. Season and mix well. Make into 8 cakes and chill for 1 hour until firm.

■ Lightly coat the cakes in flour. Heat the butter in a non-stick frying pan and cook, in batches, over a medium heat for 4–5 minutes each side until browned and heated through (don't let them burn). To make the dill sauce, mix the dill into the crème fraîche and season with salt and pepper. Serve the swede and bacon cakes with the dill sauce and a green salad. **Serves 4**

Swede is a very dense vegetable so use a heavy, sharp knife to cut it up.

# Mushroom risotto

30 minutes

**vegetable or chicken stock** fresh, cubes or
    powder, made up to 1 litre
**butter** 125g
**olive oil**
**onion** 1, finely diced
**field mushrooms or chestnut mushrooms**
    200g, diced
**risotto rice** such as carnaroli, 300g
**white wine** 75ml
**chopped chives** 1 tbsp
**Parmesan cheese** 125g, freshly grated to
    serve
**truffle oil** to serve (optional)

■ Bring the stock to a gentle simmer. In a pan, melt half of the butter with 1 tbsp olive oil. Add the onion and fry over a low heat for 3 minutes. Add the mushrooms and cook for a further 3 minutes. Add the rice and stir well, coating each grain with butter and oil. Add enough stock just to cover the rice and simmer gently, stirring frequently until the stock is absorbed. Continue stirring and adding the hot stock, waiting until each batch is absorbed before adding the next. The risotto is ready when the rice is creamy and cooked. Finally, add the wine and stir in the remaining butter and season to taste. Mix well and serve topped with chives, Parmesan and truffle oil, if you like. **Serves 4**

Carnaroli is a particularly well-behaved risotto rice but arborio also works well.

# Celeriac mash with roast chicken quarters

50 minutes

**chicken quarters** 4, skin on
**butter**
**lemon** 1, halved
**celeriac** 2, peeled and cubed
**garlic** 2 cloves, peeled
**double cream** 4 tbsp
**nutmeg** freshly grated, to season
**green vegetables** to serve

■ Heat the oven to 180°C/fan 160°C/gas 4. Put the chicken quarters on a roasting tray and season with salt and pepper. Dot with a little butter, squeeze over the lemon halves and roast for 40–50 minutes until the skin is crisp and brown and there are no red juices oozing out of the joints.

■ Meanwhile, peel and cube the celeriac, dropping it straight into a saucepan of boiling water as you do so. Add the garlic cloves and simmer for about 15 minutes until tender. Drain the celeriac and garlic and then mash them together (unlike potato, you can whiz this in a food processor without it going gluey). Beat in a large knob of butter and the cream and season with salt, pepper and nutmeg. Serve with the chicken and some green veg. **Serves 4**

Heavy, lumpy and ugly, celeriac responds well to a makeover. Mash it on its own, as here, or with an equal quantity of potato if you want a lighter, fluffier result.

# Roast loin of pork

30 minutes + 1 hour 50 minutes
in the oven

olive oil
**loin of pork** about 1.3kg, boned and rolled
(ask your butcher to do this), scored
**sea salt**
**eating apples** 3, cut into wedges
**plain flour** 1 tbsp
**vegetable or chicken stock** fresh, cube or
concentrate, made up to 400ml

If the pork skin isn't scored enough then
use a very sharp blade to add more cuts.

■ Heat the oven to 240°C/fan 220°C/gas 9.
Lightly oil a roasting tin and put it in the
oven to get hot. Season the skin of the
pork with salt, then put the joint in the
hot tin and roast for 20 minutes. Reduce
the heat to 190°C/fan 170°C/gas 5 and
roast for a further 30 minutes per 500g.
Increase the heat to 240°C/fan 220°C/gas
9 and cook for a final 10 minutes to get a
crisp and golden crackling. Take the pork
from the tin and rest in a warm place
before carving into slices.
■ Meanwhile, drain the excess fat from
the roasting tin on to a baking tray. Add
the apples to the hot fat, turn to coat
and roast for 10 minutes. Take out and
keep warm. Put the roasting tin directly
over a low heat, sprinkle in the flour and
mix well. Then slowly add the stock,
stirring until you have a gravy. Season
and sieve into a jug. Serve the pork with
the roasting apples and gravy. **Serves 4**

# Italian baked rabbit with green olives and lemon

20 minutes + 1 ½ hours in the oven

**rabbit** 1, jointed into 6–8 pieces (ask the butcher to do this)

**olive oil**

**onion** 1, finely chopped

**garlic** 2 cloves, crushed

**flat-leaf parsley** chopped, 4 tbsp

**oregano or marjoram** finely chopped, 1 tbsp

**lemons** 2, zested and juice of 1, the other cut into wedges

**green olives** pitted or whole, a handful

**potatoes** 3, cut into chunks

**white wine** 300ml

■ Heat the oven to 180°C/fan 160°C/gas 4. Brown the rabbit pieces in a little olive oil in a large, ovenproof casserole then remove. Tip in a little more oil, add the onion and fry over a low heat for a couple of minutes. Add the garlic, 2 tbsp parsley and the oregano or marjoram. Cook until an aromatic paste, then return the rabbit to the casserole.

■ Stir in the lemon zest and juice, the olives, potatoes and wine. Bring to the boil and season well. Cover with a lid and bake for 1 hour. Remove the lid and bake for a further 30 minutes to reduce the sauce a little. Stir in the remaining parsley. **Serves 4**

If you have preserved lemon in your store-cupboard, you could use 1 chopped instead of the lemon zest and juice.

# Fish pie

2 hours

**full fat milk** 500ml
**black peppercorns** 4
**parsley stalk** 1
**bay leaf** 1
**white fish fillet** 250g skinless
**smoked haddock** 250g skinless, undyed
**butter** 50g, plus some for the top
**plain flour** 1 rounded tbsp
**potatoes** 600g, peeled and cut into
    quarters
**spring onions** 4, finely chopped
**peeled Atlantic prawns** 100g
**eggs** 2, hard boiled and roughly chopped
**flat-leaf parsley** a handful, chopped

■ Heat the oven to 190°C/fan 170°C/gas 5. Bring 350ml milk, the peppercorns, parsley stalk and bay leaf to the boil. Lower the heat, add the white fish and smoked haddock, cover and gently poach for about 8 minutes or until just cooked. Remove the fish from the pan and strain the milk.

■ Melt half the butter, stir in the flour and cook for 30 seconds. Stir in the strained milk, bring to the boil, stirring as you go. Reduce heat to a very gentle simmer for about 10 minutes. Meanwhile, cook the potatoes, drain, mash until smooth and add the remaining butter, milk and the spring onions. Season and set aside.

■ Flake the fish into chunks and add to the white sauce with the prawns and egg. Season; add the parsley. Divide between 2 ovenproof dishes, top with the mash and dot with the butter. Cook for 40–45 minutes or until the top is golden and the filling is bubbling. **Serves 2**

Floury potatoes will make a fluffier mash than waxy ones.

# Belly of pork with preserved lemon and sage potatoes

20 minutes + 3–4 hours in the oven

**potatoes** 1 kg

**red onions** 3

**preserved lemon** 1

**sage** 1 very large sprig, leaves chopped

**belly of pork on the bone** 1 whole piece, about 1.6kg (ask the butcher or meat counter to score the rind for crackling)

**Dijon mustard** 3 tbsp

**clear honey** 2 tbsp

**chicken stock** fresh, powder or cube, made up to 100ml

■ Heat the oven to 150°C/fan 130°C/gas 2. Arrange the potatoes, onions, lemon and sage in layers in a roasting tin big enough to fit the pork. Season lightly as you go. Finish with a layer of potatoes then put the pork on top, skin-side up. Cook for at least 3 hours – if it stays in for 4, that's fine.

■ Increase the oven temperature to 230°C/fan 210°C/gas 8. Transfer the pork to a second roasting tin and put it back in the oven. Put the potato mixture on the shelf below. Cook for 20–30 minutes until the crackling on the pork has bubbled and is very crisp. Lift the pork back on the potatoes to rest for 10 minutes out of the oven before carving.

■ Meanwhile, to make the sauce, put the mustard, honey and stock in a small pan and simmer for 3 minutes until it is the consistency of single cream. Drizzle over each serving of pork and potato. **Serves 4**

A mandolin or slicing disc on a food processor will get the onions and potatoes thin.

# Lancashire mutton hotpot

30 minutes + 2 ¾ hours in the oven

**olive oil**

**onions** 2 large, roughly chopped

**potatoes** 800g, Desiree or Romano, sliced about the thickness of a £1 coin

**mutton or lamb chump chops** 4, or **best end of neck chops of lamb or mutton** 8–12 depending on size, trimmed

**bay leaves** 4

**thyme** 8 sprigs (optional)

**butter** melted (optional)

**pickled red cabbage or steamed green veg** to serve

You can buy mutton from some butchers or by mail order. If you prefer, you can use hill or mountain lamb that is in season now.

■ Heat the oven to 200°C/fan 180°C/gas 6. Heat a little oil in a large, heavy frying pan and fry the onion gently for at least 10 minutes until translucent and pale gold. Transfer to a plate. Add more oil to the pan if necessary and brown the chops.

■ Spread ⅔ of the potatoes in a baking dish about 7cm deep and wide enough to hold the meat in a single layer. Season. Put the chops and bay leaves on top of the potatoes and scatter on the thyme, if using. Season. Spread the onion over the meat and season again. Pour 200ml water into the frying pan, stir and scrape over the heat to release the sticky debris from the bottom. Pour into the dish, adding more water if needed, until the liquid comes halfway up the contents of the dish.

■ Cover with the remaining potatoes. Brush with more oil or melted butter. Cover with a double layer of foil and cook for 30 minutes. Turn the temperature down to 150°C/fan 130°C/gas 2 and cook for a further 2 hours, then remove the foil to brown the potato slices lightly – turning the oven back up to 180°C/fan 160°C/gas 4 to help them along. **Serves 4**

# Chicken with lemon and olives

1 hour 15 minutes

**red onions** 2, cut into eight wedges

**garlic** 6 cloves, unpeeled

**preserved (or pickled) lemon** 1 small, pulp removed and shredded **or 1 lemon** cut into thin wedges

**white wine** 250ml

**chicken** 8 pieces, a mixture of thighs, drumsticks and breasts (on the bone if possible)

**olive oil**

**pitted green olives** 100g, drained

**flat-leaf parsley** a small bunch, roughly chopped

**couscous** to serve

■ Heat the oven to 190°C/fan 170°C/gas 5. Put the onions, garlic, lemon and wine into a large casserole or ovenproof dish. Cut any excess fatty bits off the chicken then rub the pieces all over with olive oil and sit them on top of the veg and liquid. Sprinkle with salt and cook for 45 minutes. Add the olives to the pot, then cook for another 10 minutes or until the chicken is golden and cooked through.

■ Take out the chicken and leave to rest. Bubble up the pan juices on the stove for 5 minutes until reduced a little then stir through the parsley. Serve the chicken with buttered couscous and the juices.

**Serves 4**

Look for the Belazu brand of preserved lemons in supermarkets or find them in Middle Eastern shops.

# Pumpkin pizzette

**20 minutes + 20 minutes rising**

**pizza base mix** 1 packet (about 300g)
**pumpkin or butternut squash** 500g
**fresh sage leaves** 8, chopped
**olive oil**
**mozzarella or taleggio cheese** 150g,
    cut into cubes

■ Heat the oven to 200°C/fan 180°C/gas 6. Make up the pizza base and leave to rise for 20 minutes. Skin the pumpkin and slice as thinly as you can. Toss in a bowl with the sage and 4 tbsp olive oil. Season well.

■ Divide the risen dough into 2 or 4. On a lightly floured surface, roll each piece to a very thin oval. Transfer to 1 or 2 well-oiled baking sheets. Top with the pumpkin slices and cheese, then drizzle with any remaining oil and sage. Bake for 12–15 minutes until the dough is browned at the edges and the pumpkin is cooked through. **Serves 2**

You could also use the topping on a ready-made pizza base.

# Chorizo and pork with haricot beans

20 minutes + 2 ½ hours in the oven

**boneless belly pork** 750g piece, skin removed
**olive oil**
**diced pancetta** 130g
**onion** 1 large, chopped
**garlic** 2 cloves, roughly chopped
**hot smoked paprika** 1 tsp
**chorizo sausage** 200g, roughly chopped
**chopped tomatoes** 400g tin
**red wine** 150ml
**haricot or cannellini beans** 400g tin, drained and rinsed
**coriander** a bunch, roughly chopped

■ Heat the oven to 160°C/fan 140°C/gas 3. Cut the belly pork into large chunks. Heat 1 tbsp oil in a large, ovenproof casserole and fry the pork in batches over a high heat until browned all over, then remove with a slotted spoon. Add the pancetta and cook for 2–3 minutes until golden, then reduce the heat slightly and add the onion and garlic. Cook for 2–3 minutes until softened. Stir in the paprika and chorizo and cook for a minute or so.
■ Return the pork to the pan and tip in the tomatoes. Pour in the wine and enough water just to cover – about 350ml. Season, cover and cook in the oven for 2 hours. Stir in the haricot beans and return to the oven, without the lid, for 20–30 minutes. Stir in the coriander and serve with crusty bread. **Serves 6**

It is worth buying a good-quality chorizo for this. Choose a whole one rather than slices.

# Mushroom and tarragon pot pies

1 hour

---

**onion** 1 large, halved and sliced

**oil** for frying

**chestnut mushrooms** 400g, halved, or quartered if large

**frozen peas** 200g, defrosted

**tarragon** a small bunch, leaves chopped

**double cream** 142ml carton

**puff pastry** 250g, rolled out

**egg** 1, beaten

■ Fry the onion gently in a little oil until completely softened and starting to turn golden, about 10 minutes. Add the mushrooms and cook for 5–10 minutes until they are browned and any liquid has evaporated. Add the peas, cream and tarragon and bubble up for a couple of minutes. Season. Divide among 4 individual pie dishes.

■ Cut 4 puff pastry lids about 2cm bigger than the dishes. Brush the rims with egg then drape over the pastry lids and press the edges on to the dish. Brush all over with egg. Bake for 25–30 minutes until puffed and golden. **Serves 4**

You can assemble the pies the day before then chill them ready to go in the oven – just give them an extra 5 minutes cooking time.

# Succotash

20 minutes

**rindless smoked streaky bacon** 150g,
  preferably in one piece, cut into strips
**onion** 1, chopped
**butter beans** 2 × 400g tins, drained
**chicken stock** powder or cubes, made up
  to 100ml
**sweetcorn** 3 ears, cut into fat disks
**double cream** 3 tbsp
**flat-leaf parsley** a good handful, finely
  chopped

■ Put the bacon in a frying pan over a
low heat and cook until the fat starts to
run out. Turn up the heat and fry until
crisp and golden. Add the onion and cook
for about 3 minutes, until soft.

■ Add the beans and stock to the pan
and simmer gently until the stock is
reduced by half. Add the sweetcorn and
cream and simmer for 5 minutes or until
the corn is tender. Stir in the parsley.

**Serves 4**

If you want to make this out of season,
use frozen corn kernels instead of whole
cobs.

# Squidgy spiced apple cake

20 minutes + 1 hour baking

**butter** 125g

**dark muscovado sugar** 225g

**eggs** 2, lightly beaten

**plain flour** 225g

**baking powder** 2 tsp

**nutmeg** 2 tsp, freshly grated

**ground cinnamon** 1 tsp

**cooking apples** 300g, peeled, cored and diced

**clear honey** 2 tbsp

**demerara sugar** 2 tbsp

■ Heat the oven to 160°C/fan 140°C/gas 3. Cream the butter and muscovado sugar for a couple of minutes, then mix in the egg. Sift over the flour, baking powder and spices. Fold together, then stir in the apple.

■ Pour into a buttered, base-lined 20cm springform cake tin and bake for 1 hour, or until risen and browned. Combine the honey and demerara, and spread over the cake while still warm. Keeps for 3–4 days wrapped in foil. **Serves 6–8**

For a slightly lighter cake use light muscovado or light soft-brown sugar.

# Plum crumbles

35 minutes

**plums** 12, stoned and halved
**ground cinnamon** 1 tsp
**orange** 1, zest and juice
**light muscovado sugar** 100g
**butter** 125g, cut into little cubes
**flour** 150g
**rolled oats** 25g
**chopped hazelnuts** 50g
**clotted cream or ice cream** to serve

■ Heat the oven to 180°C/fan 160°C/gas 4. Put the plums, cinnamon, orange zest and juice and half of the sugar in a bowl and mix. Divide the plum mixture among 4 individual pie dishes and add 3 butter cubes to each.

■ Rub the rest of the butter into the flour until it looks like coarse sand. Stir in the remaining sugar, the oats and the hazelnuts. Sprinkle this mixture over the plums. Bake for 15–20 minutes until the juice starts to bubble through the crumbles. Serve with clotted cream or ice cream. **Serves 4**

There are several types of plum from which to choose at this time of year. Victorias are the English classic, Czar cook well, and damsons are fabulous if you can get them (although they're smaller, so double the quantity).

# Steamed blackberry pudding

15 minutes + 1 ½–2 hours steaming

**butter** 75g, at room temperature, plus some for buttering

**caster sugar** 100g

**lemon** 1, zest only

**eggs** 2, beaten

**self-raising flour** 125g

**milk** 4 tbsp

**golden syrup** 4 tbsp

**blackberries** 1 large punnet

**custard** to serve

Blackberries appear in the shops in early summer, but September is the month to go looking in the hedgerows for the wild version.

■ Butter and flour 6 × 250ml individual basins or moulds or 1/1.2 litre basin. Cream the butter, sugar and lemon zest in a large bowl with an electric hand whisk until light and fluffy. Beat in the eggs, flour and milk, then stir in 2 tbsp golden syrup. Divide the remaining golden syrup and the blackberries among the pudding basins and spoon the sponge mixture over each one. Cover each with a double piece of foil or greaseproof paper, with a pleat across the centre. Tie on firmly with a piece of string.

■ Cook in a steamer over simmering water for 40–50 minutes. Top up with water if you need to. Check the puddings are cooked with a skewer – it should come out clean. Turn out on to a plate, scooping up any blackberries left behind in the basin. Serve with custard. **Serves 6**

# Old-fashioned coffee and walnut cake

20 minutes + 25 minutes in the oven

**butter** 175g, softened
**golden caster sugar** 175g
**eggs** 3
**instant espresso coffee granules** 2 tbsp, mixed with enough boiling water to make a paste
**self-raising flour** 175g
**baking powder** 2 tsp
**walnut pieces** 50g, toasted

ICING
**unsalted butter** 150g, softened
**icing sugar** 350g, plus some for dusting
**instant espresso coffee granules** 2–3 tsp, dissolved in 1 tbsp boiling water
**walnut halves** to decorate

■ Heat the oven to 180°C/fan 160°C/gas 4. Base-line and butter 2 × 20cm sandwich tins. Cream the butter and caster sugar with electric beaters until fluffy. Beat in the eggs one by one, then the coffee, fold in the flour and baking powder. Add a little milk if the mixture is too thick (it should fall off a spoon) and then fold in the walnuts. Spoon into the sandwich tins and bake for 20–25 minutes. Cool on a wire rack.

■ Cream the butter and icing sugar (electric beaters will give more volume). Beat in the coffee a little at a time to taste. Sandwich the cooled cakes together with half the icing and then use the other half to decorate the top along with the walnut halves and a dusting of cocoa or icing sugar. **Cuts into 8**

Crack your own while walnuts are at their best – save the best ones for the top.

# Apple pie

20 minutes + 40 minutes in the oven

**Bramley apples** 6 (about 700g), peeled, cored and sliced
**caster sugar** 4 tbsp, plus some for sprinkling
**cinnamon** ½ tsp
**orange** 1, zest and juice
**butter**
**ready-roll shortcrust pastry** 350g

■ Heat the oven to 180°C/fan 160°C/gas 4. Toss the apples with the sugar, cinnamon and orange zest and juice and fill 4 small pie dishes or 1 large one. Add a knob of butter to each. Roll out the pastry and cover each pie dish. Press the edge of the pastry to the dish and trim; crimp the edges if you like. Make a couple of small cuts in the top of each and decorate with cut out pastry leaves and/or apples. Sprinkle with a little more sugar. Bake for 35–40 minutes until the pastry is dry and gold. **Serves 4**

Bramley's Seedling apples are the British cooking apple. If you fancy a bit more texture then use half Bramley and half eating apples.

# Baked pear dumplings

50 minutes

**shortcrust pastry** 500g
**pears** 4, all the same size, peeled but
　　with stalks intact
**cardamom** 4 pods, seeds only (about ¼
　　tsp seeds)
**dark muscovado sugar** 2 tbsp
**prunes or dried apricots** 8, finely chopped
**milk and golden caster sugar** to glaze

■ Heat the oven to 200°C/fan 180°C/gas 6. Divide the pastry into 4 and roll each piece into a circle about 20cm in diameter. Pull the stalk out of each pear and keep them aside. Core the pears using an apple corer or sharp knife.

■ Crush the cardamom seeds using a pestle and mortar and mix with the sugar and prunes or apricots. Put a pear upright on each pastry circle and fill the pears with the prune mixture. Brush the edges of the pastry with water and fold the pastry up around the pear, keeping the shape of the pear. Press to seal and trim off any excess. Brush with milk and sprinkle with caster sugar. If you have the inclination, make some pastry leaves and stick them to the tops of the pears. Put a reserved stalk back in each and bake on a buttered baking sheet for 30 minutes until the pastry is golden. **Serves 4**

You'll need ripe pears for this; if they seem a bit hard, peel and cook them in water, along with some sugar and a twist of orange peel, for 20 minutes first.

# Bramble syllabubs with a splash of ginger

15 minutes + chilling

**lemon** 1, zested and the juice of ½
**golden caster sugar** 4 tbsp
**bramble liqueur or crème de mûres**
    6 tbsp
**ginger wine** 2 tbsp
**double cream** 284ml carton
**blackberries and icing sugar** to decorate
**ginger thins** (biscuits) to serve

■ Put the lemon zest and juice in a large bowl with the sugar, liqueur and ginger wine, and stir until the sugar dissolves. Add the cream, a bit at a time, beating constantly with a balloon whisk. Continue beating until the mixture just holds its shape but be careful not to over-beat – syllabub goes on thickening after the beating stops.

■ Spoon into small dishes or glasses and chill (you can make these up to 24 hours in advance). Decorate with a few blackberries, dust with icing sugar, and serve with plenty of ginger thins. **Serves 4**

Look for crème de mûres from France and bramble liqueur in specialist off-licences or use crème de cassis.

# Damson slump

20 minutes + 45 minutes in the oven

**damsons** 1kg
**golden caster sugar** 200g
**self-raising flour** 125g
**milk** 125–50ml
**unsalted butter** 2 tbsp, melted

■ Heat the oven to 180°C/fan 160°C/gas 4. Divide the damsons among 4 ovenproof dishes (or use one large dish) and sprinkle evenly with 150g of the sugar. Sift the flour and add the remaining sugar to a bowl with a pinch of salt. Whisk in the butter and enough milk to make a thick, smooth mixture that will just fall off the spoon.

■ Spoon big blobs over the damsons but don't worry if the fruit is not completely covered – it will bubble through as it cooks. Bake for 40–45 minutes until the tops are golden. Leave for 20 minutes before serving. **Serves 4**

It's better to leave the stones in the damsons than to waste hours trying to extract them.

# Jumbled plum and almond tart

<u>45 minutes</u>

**ready-roll puff pastry** 375g
**plums** 750g–1kg, stoned and halved or
    quartered
**marzipan** 40g
**flaked almonds** 25g
**egg yolk** 1, beaten with 1 tbsp water
**plum jam** 6 tbsp

Use an all-butter puff pastry for a
better flavour. Jus-Rol do a frozen version
or look for Dorset organic pastry.

■ Heat the oven to 200°C/fan 180°C/gas 6.
Lay the pastry on a baking sheet and fold
in the edges as narrowly as possible, then
fold over again to make a border, pressing
lightly with a fork to seal. Pinch the
corners and give them a little twist. Prick
the base all over with the fork and chill
for 10 minutes.

■ Pack the plums closely together in the
tart case, pinching off little pieces of
marzipan and tucking them into the
gaps between the plums as you go, then
scatter over the almonds. Brush the
edges with the egg yolk mixture and
bake for 10–15 minutes until the pastry is
puffed and light gold. Turn the oven
down to 180°C/fan 160°C/gas 4 and bake
for a further 15–20 minutes until the
pastry is deep golden and the fruit soft.

■ Meanwhile, warm the plum jam and
push through a sieve into a small bowl,
then brush all over the fruit and pastry
edges to glaze before serving. **Serves 6**

# Butternut tortilla

**55 minutes (or 25 minutes if you roast the squash ahead)**

**butternut squash** about 800g
**olive oil**
**lemon thyme** 6 sprigs, leaves stripped
  and roughly chopped
**eggs** 5
**garlic** 1 clove, crushed
**ricotta cheese** 175g
**green salad** to serve

■ Heat the oven to 200°C/fan 180°C/gas 6. Trim the squash and cut into chunks. If you like a bit of a crunch, leave the skin on and some of the seeds in. Transfer to a non-stick baking sheet, drizzle with 2 tbsp olive oil, sprinkle with thyme and roast for 30 minutes. You can do this the night before if you like.

■ Put the eggs and garlic in a bowl and mix well. Season with salt and pepper. Heat a little olive oil in an ovenproof 22cm frying pan. Add the roasted squash and the egg mixture and top with blobs of ricotta. Cook in the oven for 15 minutes until set. Leave to rest for 5 minutes. Serve with a green salad. **Serves 4**

If you have time, firm up your ricotta by draining it in a sieve overnight.

# Celeriac soup with white beans and lemon oil

25 minutes

olive oil

onion 1, sliced

chicken or vegetable stock cubes or
    powder, made up to 750ml

celeriac 1, about 500g

white beans (such as cannellini or butter
    beans) 410g can, rinsed and drained

fresh flat-leaf parsley 4 tbsp chopped,
    reserve some for the garnish

lemon-flavoured olive oil to garnish

■ Heat 1 tbsp olive oil in a saucepan and fry the onion for 2 minutes until softened but not browned. Add the stock to the onion and leave over a low heat. Peel and cube the celeriac. To prevent it from discolouring, add it to the stock as you chop. Bring to the boil, cover and simmer for 15 minutes until soft.

■ Add half the beans to the soup, then whiz in a blender. Pour back into the pan and add the parsley and remaining beans. Add a little more water if it seems too thick. Season well with salt and pepper.

■ Ladle into bowls. Before serving, drizzle with a little lemon oil and sprinkle with parsley and freshly milled black pepper.

Serves 4

Lemon-flavoured olive oil is a great way to add flavour without the bother of grating lemon zest.

# Winter warmer soup

30 minutes

**onions** 2, finely chopped
**garlic** 2 cloves, peeled and chopped
**bacon lardons** 200g
**olive oil**
**parsnips** 4, finely chopped
**thyme sprigs** 2
**red chillies** 2, finely chopped
**vegetable stock** cubes or powder, made
    up to 2 litres
**Brussels sprouts** 500g, finely sliced

■ Put the onions, garlic and lardons in a large saucepan, drizzle with a little oil and cook over a medium heat for 6 minutes, stirring. Add the parsnips, thyme, chillies and stock, bring to the boil, then simmer for 15 minutes.

■ Just before serving, add the sprouts, season with a little sea salt and freshly milled black pepper and simmer for 5 minutes. Serve with grilled toast with goat's cheese on top. **Serves 8**

Cabbage could replace the Brussels sprouts, but won't be as sweet. If you make ahead, add the sprouts just before eating, to keep their vibrant colour.

# Baked Brie in puff pastry with cranberries

**30 minutes + 30 minutes in the oven + chilling**

**fresh or frozen cranberries** 500g
**redcurrant jelly** 4 tbsp
**light muscovado sugar** 150g
**brandy** 2 tbsp
**port** 1 tbsp
**ready-roll puff pastry** 350g pack
**Brie cheese** 1 wheel (about 1kg), chilled until very firm
**egg yolk** 1

Serve with a green salad for a winter lunch.

■ Put the cranberries, redcurrant jelly, sugar and both measures of alcohol in a saucepan and bring to a simmer. Cook for about 10 minutes, stirring frequently, until thickened. Cool. This sauce can be made 1 week ahead – store in the fridge.

■ Roll out the pastry on a lightly floured surface until it is large enough to wrap the Brie. Place the Brie in the centre of the pastry and top with 2 tbsp of the cranberry sauce (use the rest on Christmas Day or with cold cuts). Bring edges of pastry together in the middle and crimp until sealed. Trim off excess pastry. Carefully turn the parcel over and place on a large baking sheet. Cut out decorative leaves from the left-over pastry, brush with water and stick on the pastry top. Chill for at least 30 minutes before baking.

■ Heat the oven to 190°C/fan 170°C/gas 5. Mix the egg yolk with 1 tbsp water and brush all over the pastry. Bake for 25-30 minutes or until golden brown. Remove from the oven and let it stand for 10 minutes before serving. **Serves 12**

# Oysters with Thai chilli butter

**10 minutes**

oysters 12, shucked (opened)
butter 50g
fish sauce 1 tbsp
root ginger 1cm piece, grated
red chillies 2, seeded and finely chopped
lime 1, zest and juice
golden caster sugar 1 tsp
coriander leaves a handful, chopped

■ Arrange the oysters on the half shell on a platter. Put the butter, fish sauce, ginger, chilli, lime and sugar in a small saucepan and heat gently for 2–3 minutes until the butter and sugar have melted and are bubbling. Drizzle over the oysters and sprinkle the coriander over the top. **Serves 2**

Pick up the oysters on your way home. If you're very organised, call the fishmonger ahead and ask him to open them for you.

# Venison steaks with berry and juniper sauce

40 minutes

**venison steaks** 8, about 200g each

**oil** for brushing

**juniper berries** 2 tsp, crushed

**red wine** 200ml

**beef or chicken stock** cubes or powder, made up to 250ml

**redcurrant jelly** 200g

**frozen redcurrants or cranberries** thawed, to serve

■ Brush each venison steak with a little oil and rub with crushed juniper berries (saving a little for the sauce), sea salt and freshly milled black pepper. To make the sauce, put the wine in a pan and add the stock and remaining crushed juniper berries. Bring to the boil and simmer for 8–10 minutes until reduced and slightly syrupy. Stir in the redcurrant jelly and heat gently until it all melts in. Season to taste. Keep warm.

■ Cook the steaks in batches in a hot griddle pan or heavy frying pan for 2 minutes on each side for rare (3 minutes for medium, 4 minutes for well done). Keep each batch warm as you cook the rest. Serve the venison steaks with the sauce and a sprig each of redcurrants or some cranberries. **Serves 8**

Bring the venison steaks to room temperature to get your cooking times more accurate.

# Roast butternut squash with chorizo

**20 minutes + 1 hour in the oven**

olive oil

**butternut squash** 2, about 600g each, halved lengthways and seeds removed

**rosemary** 4 sprigs, leaves stripped and chopped

**garlic bulb** 1, halved horizontally

**chorizo sausages** 8 small, cut into ½cm slices

**Manchego cheese** 300g, diced

■ Heat the oven to 220°C/fan 200°C/gas 7. Put a large piece of lightly oiled foil on a baking sheet and lay 2 squash halves on top, cut-side up. Drizzle with olive oil and season generously with salt and pepper. Scatter over half the rosemary and tuck in a garlic half. Make a loose parcel with the foil. Repeat the process with the second squash. Bake until tender, about 45 minutes. If making ahead of time, allow the squash to cool and chill for up to 2 days.

■ Open the foil parcel, push the garlic to one side and divide the cheese and chorizo among the 4 halves. Re-wrap and cook for 15 minutes. Serve cut into slices along with the garlic if you like. **Serves 6**

For a veggie version, leave out the chorizo and add some diced, lightly fried courgette instead.

# Spiced lamb cutlets with jewelled couscous

20 minutes + marinating

**garlic** 6 cloves, crushed with 2 tsp sea salt
**ground cinnamon** 2 tsp
**ground allspice** 2 tsp
**olive oil**
**lemon** 1, juiced
**lamb cutlets** 12, excess fat removed

COUSCOUS

**couscous** 500g
**butter** 50g
**pomegranate** 1
**flaked almonds** 100g, toasted
**ground cinnamon** 2 tsp
**coriander** a small handful, chopped
**mint** a small handful, chopped

■ Mix the garlic, spices, 4 tbsp olive oil and lemon juice to form a paste. Rub over the cutlets and leave to marinate for at least 2 hours or overnight.

■ Put the couscous and butter in a shallow bowl. Add 500ml boiling water and 2 tsp sea salt, cover and stand until the liquid has been absorbed (about 5 minutes). Cut the pomegranate in half and remove the seeds. Fluff the couscous with a fork and add the almonds, cinnamon and pomegranate seeds. Stir in the herbs and season.

■ Grill the lamb cutlets under a high heat for 4 minutes on each side. Serve with the couscous. **Serves 6**

Roll the pomegranate across the kitchen counter, pressing down firmly to loosen the seeds, before you cut it open.

# Beef carbonade

35 minutes + 2 hours 40 minutes in
the oven

**olive oil**

**butter** 50g

**onions** 6, sliced

**braising steak** 1.5kg, cut into chunks

**flour** 3 tbsp, seasoned

**brown ale** 900ml

**light muscovado sugar** 1 tbsp

**white wine vinegar** 2 tsp

**French bread** 6 slices

**Dijon mustard** to taste

You can make this ahead, up to the point
where you add the bread if you like. To
finish, bring it to a simmer before adding
the bread, then follow the recipe again.

■ Heat the oven to 150°C/fan 130°C/gas 2.
Heat 1 tbsp oil and most of the butter in
a frying pan and fry onions until tender
but not coloured. Place in a large
casserole dish. Toss the beef in 2 tbsp
flour and shake off excess. Heat 1 tbsp oil
in the same pan and brown beef in
batches. Add to dish.

■ Swirl out the pan with half the ale and
pour over the beef and onions. Add the
remaining ale to the casserole and bring
to the boil. Season, cover and cook in the
oven for 2 hours or until the meat is
tender. With a slotted spoon remove the
beef and onions and set aside. Form a
paste with the remaining flour and 1 tbsp
butter. Bring casserole liquid to a gentle
boil and stir in a little paste at a time,
until thickened slightly. Add sugar and
vinegar.

■ Return meat and onions to the
casserole. Spread the bread slices with
Dijon mustard and arrange on top of the
beef. Return the casserole to the oven
uncovered for a further 35–40 minutes.
Serve with mash and greens. **Serves 6**

# Roast turkey with caramelised shallots

2 hours (depending on size of bird)
+ resting time

**olive oil**
**shallots** 500g, peeled and finely sliced (or use onions)
**sage** 5 leaves, chopped
**butter** 50g, softened
**turkey** 4–6kg, untrussed
**red wine** 400ml

Tie the turkey legs together if you want a neater look, as in the picture opposite.

■ Heat 1 tbsp oil in a frying pan and gently cook the shallots with 1 tsp salt for about 20 minutes, stirring until soft and dark brown. Stir in the sage and add black pepper. Cool, then mix with the butter. Ease your fingers under the turkey skin from the neck end – loosening it over the breast and thighs – and spread the shallot butter under the skin. Sprinkle all over with sea salt.

■ Heat the oven to 180°C/fan 160°C/gas 4. Put the turkey in a roasting tin and roast for 22 minutes per kilo. For the last 45 minutes, turn the heat up to 200°C/fan 180°C/gas 6. Test by pushing a skewer into the thigh: the juices should run clear. Put on a serving dish, cover with foil, and rest for 20 minutes to an hour.

■ Meanwhile, make the gravy. Spoon off the fat from the roasting-tin juices. Put the tin on the heat and add the wine, stirring and scraping the bottom of the pan with a wooden spoon. Simmer for a couple of minutes. Season. Sieve into a gravy jug and serve with the turkey.

**Serves 8**

# Duck with berry sauce and baked celeriac

2 hours

**butter**
**celeriac** 750g, peeled and thinly sliced
**double cream** 284ml carton
**whole milk** 150ml
**Parmesan cheese** 25g, grated
**Merlot or other red wine** 100ml
**crème de cassis** 2 tbsp
**beef stock** fresh, cube or powder, made
  up to 50ml
**arrowroot** 1 tsp, mixed with 1 tbsp cold
  water
**mixed frozen berries** (such as raspberries,
  blueberries, blackcurrants or
  blackberries) 125g
**duck breasts** 2, skin on

■ Heat the oven to 150°C/fan 130°C/gas 2.
Butter a large, ovenproof baking dish.
Layer the celeriac, generously seasoning
with salt and pepper. Mix together the
cream and milk and pour over so it
comes up nearly to the top of the dish.
Scatter with Parmesan. Cook for 2 hours
on a baking sheet to catch any drips.
■ To make the sauce, put the wine, cassis
and stock in a pan. Bring to the boil and
simmer for 3 minutes. Stir in the arrowroot
mixture, bring to the boil again, then stir
in the berries until heated through.
■ Heat a heavy-base frying pan over a
high heat. Season the skin of the duck
with salt and pepper and cook skin-side
down. Turn the heat down to medium and
for the next 10 minutes let the duck sizzle
in its melting fat. Flip it over and cook for
another 5 minutes. Transfer to a plate to
rest while you reheat the sauce if
necessary and serve the celeriac. Slice the
duck and drizzle the sauce around. **Serves 2**

You could use cranberries instead of the
mixed berries.

# Roast rib of beef with red wine gravy

20 minutes + 1 hour 10 minutes in the oven

fennel 1 bulb, roughly chopped

celery ½ bunch, roughly chopped

carrots 3, roughly chopped

onions 2, roughly chopped

red wine 1 bottle (750ml)

beef stock fresh, cube or powder, made up to 500ml

rib of beef about 1.5k, off the bone and rolled

■ Heat the oven to 220°C/fan 200°C/gas 7. Brown the veg in a sturdy roasting dish on the hob then pour in the wine and stock and season. Sit the beef on top, transfer to the oven and cook for 30 minutes. Reduce the temperature to 200°C/fan 180°C/gas 6 and cook for 12 minutes per 500g for nicely pink. Rest for 15 minutes while you finish the gravy.

■ Strain the liquid into a pan, squeezing any juices out of the veg, and bubble for a few minutes to reduce. Serve with the beef. Any juices that come out of the meat should be added to the gravy.

**Serves 6**

Bring the beef up to room temperature before cooking it to make sure the timing is accurate.

# Turkey and tarragon pot pies

50 minutes

**onion** 1, halved and sliced

**chestnut mushrooms** 100g, quartered

**butter**

**chicken stock** fresh, cube or concentrate, made up to 300ml

**cooked turkey or chicken**, 400g, torn into chunks

**frozen peas** 100g, defrosted

**tarragon** a small bunch, leaves chopped

**double cream** 142ml carton

**ready-roll puff pastry** 2 sheets of fresh or frozen, cut to fit 4 pie dishes

**egg** 1, beaten for glazing

■ Heat the oven to 200°C/fan 180°C/gas 6. Cook the onion and mushrooms in a little butter until soft. Add the rest of the ingredients (except the pastry and eggs), bubble up and season. Divide among 4 small, ovenproof pie dishes, cover each with a circle of puff pastry and glaze with the beaten egg. Bake for 20–25 minutes until puffed and golden. **Serves 4**

Keep the turkey in bite-size chunks to give a good texture to the pie filling.

# Beef in Guinness with fluffy herb dumplings

40 minutes + 30 hours in the oven

oil

**braising steak** 1kg, cut into large pieces

**plain flour** 2 tbsp, well seasoned

**onions** 3, sliced

**Guinness** 500ml

**thyme** 2 sprigs

**Savoy cabbage** to serve

DUMPLINGS

**butter** 75g, frozen and grated

**self-raising flour** 150g

**onion** 1 small, grated

**thyme** 2 sprigs, leaves stripped and chopped

■ Heat the oven to 150°C/fan 130°C/gas 2. Heat a little oil in a large casserole pan. Dust the meat with flour and fry in batches until well browned then scoop out. Tip in the onions and fry on a fairly high heat until they begin to soften and brown at the edges.

■ Add the Guinness and let it bubble up then return the meat to the pan along with the thyme. Cover and transfer to the oven for 2–2 ½ hours or until tender.

■ Make the dumplings (once the meat has cooked) by mixing the butter, flour, onion and thyme together and season. Gradually add 6 tbsp water to the dry ingredients until you have a soft dough. Divide into 12 balls. Put the dumplings on top of the casserole and return to the oven, uncovered, for 25 minutes. Serve with shredded Savoy cabbage. **Serves 4**

Keep the dumplings as light as possible by using the blade of a knife for mixing.

# Sticky Calvados pork chops

30 minutes

**potatoes** 500g Maris Piper or King
Edward, peeled
**milk** 50ml, hot
**butter**
**chives** a small bunch, snipped
**apples** 2, sliced through the middle into
circles (no need to core them)
**sugar** 1 tsp
**pork chops** 2, dusted with 1 tsp plain
flour
**shallots** 6, thinly sliced
**Calvados** 5 tbsp
**apple juice** 125ml
**crème fraîche** 125g
**watercress** to serve

■ Boil the potatoes until tender. Drain
well and mash with the hot milk and a
knob of butter. Stir in the chives. Keep
warm. Fry the apple slices sprinkled with
sugar in a little butter for about 3
minutes each side until golden. Keep
warm.

■ Heat some butter in a large frying pan
over a medium heat. Fry the pork chops
for 6 minutes on one side, then turn and
cook for 4 minutes on the other side.
Remove and keep warm.

■ Add the shallots to the frying pan and
cook until soft. Pour in the Calvados –
stand back as it will splutter. Stir in the
apple juice, then let simmer until
reduced and slightly caramelised at the
edges. Stir in the crème fraîche, add the
chops and heat through. Season. Serve
the pork with the chive mash and apple
slices. **Serves 2**

Make snips in the fat and rind of the
chops with a pair of scissors to stop them
curling up.

# Beef and vegetable casserole

2 hours

olive oil
**onion** 1, diced
**carrot** 1, diced
**leek** 1, diced
**celery** 2 sticks, diced
**garlic** 2 cloves, crushed
**mushrooms** 75g, sliced
**braising steak** 500g, cubed
**plain flour** 2 tbsp
**thyme** 3 sprigs
**beef stock** fresh, cube or concentrate,
　　made up to 750ml
**tomato purée** 2 tbsp
**Worcestershire sauce** a dash
**jacket potatoes, rice, pasta, or mash** to
　　serve

■ Heat 1 tbsp olive oil in a large casserole then add the onion, carrot, leek, celery and garlic, and cook gently for 5 minutes. Do not brown. Add the mushrooms and cook everything for a further 5 minutes then remove from the pan. Heat a little more olive oil in the pan, add the beef (in batches if necessary) and brown all over then stir the flour in well.

■ Return the veg to the pan and add the thyme, stock, tomato, purée and Worcestershire sauce. Season and mix well. Bring to a gentle simmer and cook covered for 1 ½ hours until tender, stirring occasionally. Serve with jacket potatoes, rice, pasta or mash. **Serves 4**

Long, slow cooking means the vegetables almost dissolve into this casserole, making it richer. It tastes even better if made the day before.

# Chard with anchovy sauce and breadcrumbs

20 minutes

**sourdough or French bread** 100g, coarsely chopped in a food processor

**olive oil**

**chard** 500g

**garlic** 2 cloves, thinly sliced

**anchovy** 1, rinsed and chopped

**sultanas** 3 tbsp, soaked in boiling water for 5 minutes

**pine nuts** 2 tbsp, toasted

**sherry vinegar** 2 tbsp

**honey** 1 tsp

■ Heat the oven to 190°C/fan 170°C/gas 5. Toss the breadcrumbs with 2 tbsp olive oil and some seasoning. Spread out on a baking sheet and bake for about 5 minutes until crisp.

■ Bring a large pan of water to the boil with 2 tbsp salt. Remove the stalks from the chard and chop them into short lengths. Then chop the leaves into a similar size and keep them separate. Simmer the stalks for about 4 minutes – and then add the leaves for a minute. Drain and rinse well in cold water.

■ Heat 5 tbsp olive oil in a pan with the garlic and anchovy until the garlic is golden and the anchovy melted, then add the sultanas, pine nuts, vinegar and honey. Stir, add the chard and warm through. Sprinkle with the toasted breadcrumbs and serve immediately.

**Serves 4**

Chard comes in different colours. Look for varieties with pink, yellow and red stems.

# Brussels sprouts with hazelnuts and brown butter

20 minutes

**Brussels sprouts** 750g small, trimmed
**butter** 50g
**blanched hazelnuts** 50g, roughly chopped

■ Bring a large pan of salted water to the boil. Cook the sprouts for about 5 minutes until just done. Drain well and tip into a warmed serving dish.

■ Meanwhile, melt the butter in a small frying pan and add the hazelnuts. Cook until the hazelnuts start to brown, and the butter turns a deep golden brown and smells nutty. Tip the mixture over the sprouts, and grind some pepper on top. **Serves 8**

Larger sprouts will cook quicker if you cut a cross into the base.

# Slow-cooked red cabbage with sausages

1 hour 30 minutes

**olive oil**
**cocktail sausages** 300g, good quality
**red onion** 1, finely sliced
**red cabbage** 1kg, thinly sliced
**dark muscovado sugar** 3 tbsp
**red wine** 250ml
**chilli sauce**
**soured cream or crème fraîche** 250ml,
to serve

■ Heat 2 tbsp oil in a large pan and brown the sausages all over. Add the onions and cook until softened. Then tip in the cabbage, sugar, red wine, a pinch of salt and a shake of chilli sauce. Cover the pan and lower the heat. Cook gently for about an hour, stirring occasionally, until the cabbage is soft.

■ For the last few minutes, take the lid off the pan and raise the heat to boil down the juices so they just coat the cabbage. Season. (You can make this a couple of days ahead and reheat it gently before serving.) Pass around soured cream or crème fraîche so everyone can put a splodge on their cabbage. **Serves 8**

Using a mandolin to slice the cabbage will shred it nice and finely.

# Poached cinnamon pears with sorbet

45 minutes

**cinnamon stick** 1, broken into shards
**Muscat or other dessert wine** 1 bottle
  (750ml)
**sugar** 75g
**clear honey** 2 tbsp
**pears** 6, peeled, stalks intact
**good-quality sorbet or ice cream** to serve

■ Put the cinnamon, wine, sugar and honey in a large saucepan and heat gently. Add the pears and simmer for 30 minutes. Remove the pears to a serving dish and simmer the remaining liquid gently for about ½ an hour until it becomes a syrup. Set aside to cool.

■ Garnish each pear with a shard of cinnamon. Serve with scoops of sorbet or ice cream and drizzle with syrup. Keep any remaining syrup to serve with ice cream. **Serves 6**

If you make this the day before, all the flavours will infuse more strongly.

# Instant apple tarts

15 minutes

red-skinned dessert apples 3 small
fruit bread or brioche 4 large or 8 small
    slices
unsalted butter ¼ of a 250g packet
ground cinnamon 1–2 tsp
light muscovado sugar 4 tsp
vanilla pod 2, cut in half and then halved
    lengthways
ice cream, cream or custard to serve

■ Heat the oven to 200°C/fan 180°C/gas 6.
Core and quarter the apples. Slice thinly.
Trim the bread into 8 rectangles (if using
4 large slices, cut in half) and generously
butter one side of each. Put on a baking
sheet butter-side up.

■ Arrange the apple slices on the bread
and sprinkle with cinnamon and sugar.
Dot with the remaining butter and top
with the vanilla pods. Bake for 6 minutes
until the apples are just cooked and the
bread toasted. Serve with ice cream,
cream or custard. **Serves 4**

Worcester Pearmain and Laxton apples
look best, but any dessert apple will do.
For a patisserie-like finish, brush with
honey when cooked.

# Sticky date pudding

15 minutes + 30 minutes in the oven

**dates** 275g, pitted and chopped
**whisky** 60ml
**butter** 125g
**sugar** 125g
**eggs** 2
**self-raising flour** 125g
**cream or ice cream** to serve

SAUCE
**butter** 150g
**dark muscovado sugar** 200g
**double cream** 250ml

■ Heat the oven to 190°C/fan 170°C/gas 5. Put the dates in a saucepan with the whisky and 150ml water. Bring to the boil, then leave dates to soak until cool.
■ Cream the butter and sugar. Beat in the eggs one at a time, stir in the flour, then the date mixture. Pour into a buttered brownie tin 22cm square. Bake for 30 minutes until cooked through (test with a skewer).
■ For the sauce, put the butter, muscovado sugar and cream in a saucepan and bring slowly to the boil, stirring, then simmer for 3 minutes. Cut into squares and pour over the sauce. Serve with cream or ice cream. Cuts into 9–12 squares. **Serves 9–12**

For a chunkier texture, leave the dates halved rather than chopping them.

# Christmas pudding muffins

30 minutes

brandy 2 tbsp

Christmas pudding 200g, broken into
     lumps

plain flour 250g

baking powder 2 tsp

caster sugar 100g

milk 200ml

egg 1

unsalted butter 75g, softened

icing sugar to dust

redcurrants or glacé cherries to serve

■ Heat the oven to 180°C/fan 160°C/gas 4.
Pour the brandy over the Christmas pud.
Sift together the flour and baking
powder, add the rest of the ingredients
(except the icing sugar and cherries) and
mix into a lumpy batter.

■ Pour into a lined 16-hole mini tin and
bake for 10–15 minutes. Cool. Dust with
icing sugar and top with a redcurrant or
glacé cherry. **Makes 36**

This mixture will make 12 normal-size
muffins.

# Steamed toffee-apple pudding

**15 minutes + 1 ½–2 hours steaming**

**butter** 100g, at room temperature

**plain flour** to dust

**golden syrup** 6 tbsp

**apples** 4, peeled, cored and cut into small cubes

**golden caster sugar** 100g

**lemon** 1, zested

**eggs** 2, beaten

**self-raising flour** 125g

**milk** 4 tbsp

**custard** to serve

If you use a cooking apple like a Bramley the toffee-apple mixture will turn into a purée.

■ Butter and lightly flour a 1.2-litre pudding basin. Melt 4 tbsp of the golden syrup with 25g of the butter in a frying pan. Let it all bubble together then add the apple and cook for a further 5 minutes. Beat together the rest of the butter, the sugar and lemon zest in a large bowl with an electric whisk until pale and fluffy. Beat in the eggs, self-raising flour and milk, then stir in the rest of the golden syrup.

■ Put the toffee-apple mixture into the pudding basin and spoon over the flour mixture. Cover with a double piece of foil or greaseproof paper, with a pleat across the centre. Tie on firmly with string. Cook in a steamer over simmering water for 1½–2 hours. Top up the water if you need to. The pudding is cooked when a skewer inserted into the middle comes out clean. Turn out on to a plate, scooping up any toffee apple that gets left behind in the basin. Serve with custard. **Serves 6**

# Chocolate soufflés

30 minutes

**dark chocolate** 200g, chopped
**butter** 150g, cut into cubes plus extra for
    the ramekins
**eggs** 6
**caster sugar** 175g
**plain flour** 125g
**cream** to serve

■ Heat the oven to 180°C/fan 160°C/gas 4. Butter 6 medium ramekins. Melt the chocolate with the butter in a bowl over simmering water or in a microwave. Beat the eggs with the sugar until they are very light and fluffy and then fold in the flour.

■ Fold in the chocolate mixture and divide among the ramekins (fridge at this point if you are making ahead). Bake for 8–12 minutes. The soufflés should rise and form a firm crust, but you want them still to be slightly runny in the middle. Serve with cream. **Serves 6**

These melting chocolate puddings are much sturdier than ordinary soufflés and will behave even if made ahead and stored in the fridge until you need them.

# Index

# Picture credits and recipe credits

BBC Books would like to thank the following for providing photographs. While every effort has been made to trace and acknowledge all photographers, we would like to apologize should there be any errors or omissions.

Peter Campbell Saunders p179; Peter Cassidy p21, p55, p61, p71, p87, p93, p103, p123, p137, p151, p153, p165, p171, p183, p203; Dan Duchars p23; Gus Filgate p17, p65, p111, p145, p169, p175, p177, p185, p207; Myles New p6, p19, p29, p45, p51, p83, p85, p181, p197, p199, p211; Martin Thompson p11; David Munns p13, p15, p25, p27, p69, p95; Noel Murphy p5 (right), p163, p167, p173, p201; Roger Stowell p4 (left), p31, p33, p47, p49, p59, p67, p79, p81, p91, p105; Debi Treloar p75, p101, p109, p125, p193; Simon Walton p5 (left), p63, p135, p141, p187; Philip Webb p4 (right), p37, p39, p41, p43, p53, p57, p73, p77, p89, p97, p99, p107, p112, p115, p117, p119, p121, p126, p129, p131, p133, p139, p143, p147, p149, p195, p205; Simon Wheeler p35, p155, p157, p159, p161, p189, p191, p209.

All the recipes in this book have been created by the editorial team at BBC *olive* magazine.